Systems Literacy

© Bildungshaus St. Magdalena

Seminarhotel St. Magdalena, Linz

Mary C. Edson
Gary S. Metcalf
Peter Tuddenham
Gerhard . Chroust
(eds.)

Systems Literacy

Proceedings of the

Eighteenth IFSR Conversation 2016

St. Magdalena Linz, Austria

Bibliografische Information der Deutschen Nationalbibliothek:
Die Deutsche Nationalbibliothek verzeichnet diese Publikation in der
Deutschen Nationalbibliografie; detaillierte bibliografische Daten sind im
Internet über http://dnb.dnb.de abrufbar.

© 2017 International Federation for Systems Research (IFSR)
www.ifsr.org

Schriftenreihe SEA-Publications SEA-SR 47
Johannes Kepler University, Linz

The Conversation took place April 3-8, 2016
in St. Magdalena, Linz, Austria

Printing sponsored by the
International Federation for Systems Research (IFSR)

Herstellung und Verlag:
BoD – Books on Demand, Norderstedt, Deutschland
ISBN: 978-3-7431-7913-4

- Welcome by the Vice Rector ... 1
- *Executive Summaries from the Teams at the Conversation* ... 2
  - Systems Literacy - The Focal Theme for the IFSR Conversation ... 3
  - Team 1: Exploring Transdisciplinarity using Hierarchy Theory, Boulding's Skeleton of Science, and General Systems Theory ... 4
  - Team 2: Unity in Diversity – Making the Implicit Explicit ... 7
  - Team 3: Systems Research Team - Exploring the Relationship of Systems Research to Systems Literacy ... 9
  - List of Participants of the Conversation ... 14
- *Systems Literacy (Peter Tuddenham)* ... 15
- *Team 1: Exploring Transdisciplinarity using Hierarchy Theory, Boulding's Skeleton of Science, and General Systems Theory* ... 23
  - Motivation: Integration across Disciplines to Transdisciplinarity ... 23
  - Boulding's Skeleton (or Typology) of Science ... 26
  - Using Hierarchy Theory to move toward Transdisciplinarity ... 27
  - An Elaboration of Boulding's Typology: The rICE Seed for Social Systems Renewal ... 28
  - Core Principles from this Framework ... 29
  - Pickup, Throughput, Output, and Links to Boulding ... 31
  - Links to Hierarchy Theory and Transdisciplinarity ... 32
  - Towards A New Approach to Social System Change: A Seed for Systemic Renewal ... 33
  - Follow On Work ... 35
  - Conclusions of the Conversation and Further Development of Work ... 36
- *Team 2: Unity in Diversity – Making the Implicit Explicit* ... 38
  - Overview ... 38
  - Part 1 - The initial proposal (with some later amendments) ... 39
  - Part 2: The Conversation process ... 43
  - Part 3 – Individual Members' Reflections ... 48
    - Brigitte Daniel Allegro - Reflections ... 48
    - Gary Robert Smith: Reflections on Linz ... 49
    - Gordon Dyer: Personal Reflection on Team 2 ... 52
    - Gerhard Chroust's Retrospective: The Conversation that was not ... 52
    - Florian Daniel : Linz Conversation feedback ... 54
    - Maria Stella LOBO: Weaving impressions from the IFSR conversation in Linz ... 56
    - Xijin Tang : Individual reflections on the IFSR Conversation 2016 ... 59
- *Team 3: Systems Research Team: A Foundation for Systems Literacy* ... 64
  - Introduction: Systems Literacy as the Bridge from Sensibility to Capability ... 65
  - Exigency of Systems Research to Systems Literacy ... 66

Process Model 67
Systems Analysis – Future Potentials 68
Eight Critical Factors 69
Knowledge Base of a Discipline 71
Systems Landscape and Systemic Sensibilities 73
Shadow Side of Systems - Systems Ethics 73
Looking Ahead and Moving Forward 74
Conclusions and Recommendations 75

Toward a System of Systems Science Research & Education (George Mobus) 77

Abstract 77
The Status of Systems Science in the Social Milieu 77
My Thinking Stimulated 78
    The Linz Results from My Perspective 79
    Method 80
Systems Analysis Overview 80
Application to the Proposed SRT Proposed Process 82
    Establishing the Context 82
    The Big Picture – The Human Social System in the Ecos 83
    The Human Social System Delineated 84
    The Science & Engineering Subsystem Delineated 85
    The Normal Science Process 85
Integrating the Model with the SRT Flow of Influence Model 87
Analysis of the LoSK Process 88
    Structural and Functional Deconstruction 88
    Background on Deriving Systemese 91
Next Steps 92

What are IFSR Conversations? 94
What is the IFSR? 96

Past officers of the IFSR 97

Welcome by the Vice Rector

JKU
JOHANNES KEPLER
UNIVERSITY LINZ

Univ.-Prof. Dr. Alexander
Egyed M.Sc.
Vice Rector of Research

P +43 732 2468 3170
alexander.egyed@jku.at

Ladies and Gentlemen, dear participants of the IFSR Conversation 2016 here in Linz!

As the Vice Rector for Research of the Johannes Kepler University, it is my pleasure to open this academic event. We are delighted to have you here to participate and share in this event.

System Sciences is a holistic discipline – it unites nearly all areas of science and technology from mechatronics to informatics, from mathematics to cybernetics, from social sciences to philosophy, and beyond. System Sciences is interdisciplinary in its very nature and it thrives from the many people that contribute to it.

In that spirit, I am happy to welcome you back to St. Magdalena in Linz. This is not the first time the IFSR Conversations have been held here and my special thanks go to the organizing committee for once again selecting our city for this prestigious event: the president Gary S. Metcalf, the secretary general Gerhard Chroust, and the vice presidents Mary C. Edson, Stefan Blachfellner, and Nam Nguyen.

The Johannes Kepler University and Linz will do its best to make sure this will be another memorable event and I wish you the very best success for your deliberations in the coming week.

Univ.-Prof. Dr. Alexander Egyed M.Sc., Vice Rector of Research

JOHANNES KEPLER
UNIVERSITY LINZ
Altenberger Str. 69
4040 Linz, Austria
www.jku.at
DVR 0093696

Opening:
Mary C. Edson, Gerhard Chroust, Vice Rector Prof. Alexander Egyed, Gary S. Metcalf (l-to-r)

Executive Summaries from the Teams at the Conversation

This past April, three teams of systems scientists gathered for the 18th Biennial IFSR Conversation (formerly Fuschl Conversation) in Linz, Austria. The Conversation was held once again at Bildungshaus Sankt Magdalena, a seminar hotel on the outskirts of Linz, along the River Danube. Johannes Kepler University is just a little over a mile or kilometer away. Systems Literacy, guided by Peter Tuddenham, was the overarching theme for this Conversation. A total of 25 participants dispersed among three teams focused on these topics:

Team 1: Application of Boulding's Skeleton of Science to Inform Transdisciplinarity,
Team 2: Unity in Diversity – Making the Implicit Explicitly, and
Team 3: Exploring the Relationship of Systems Research to Systems Literacy.

Each team was asked to submit soon after the Conversation a short Management Summary. These summaries you find below. Later in the year the 3 teams Peter Tuddenham produced extensive Reports about their work. A personal reflection on the Conversation was delivered by George Mobus.

Those participants who are new and unfamiliar with the Conversation's design may be daunted by the idea of spending five days in small groups focused on singular topics, especially if they are accustomed to traditional academic conferences in which the formal lecture, unidirectional, rather than interactive and participatory. Feedback from participants tells us that while that unsettling feeling exists on Sunday, it evaporates quickly by mid-week. By Friday, most participants wonder where the week went because there is a sense that there hasn't been enough time to explore all the material that emerged from the week's Conversation. Here are some of the participants' overall impressions from this Conversation:

"...possibly the most important work in the world. Needs acceleration."
"...unsure what to expect. I had a chance to explore questions of interest to me."
"...it was a fruitful week with rich experience."
"...I can't wait until the next one!!!"
"...brainstorming process with creative/critical thinking."

Most of the participants enjoyed the collegiality and diversity of the teams. They also expressed that there is neither time nor the conditions for deep development of these subjects discussed in day-to-day academic - professional - career - work environments. The quality of interactions at this level received high marks for generativity and innovation, especially for collaboration and "co-creating knowledge," as one participant remarked. As most social interactions continue to evolve into the 21st century globally, so must the Conversation. Several participants remarked about leveraging technology and social media to enrich the discussions. We will research these options, along with several other suggestions for improvements, in the months preceding the 19th Biennial Conversation. In the meantime, we ask our member societies to encourage their members to start thinking about topic proposals and to develop ideas with colleagues who may be interested in joining the Conversation in 2018.

Systems Literacy - The Focal Theme for the IFSR Conversation
(Peter Tuddenham)

In November 2015, the 2016 IFSR Conversation team leaders met to discuss the possibility of developing an overarching theme for the 2016 Conversation. Because the teams had been articulating systemic concepts and principles, several ideas for a central theme were considered. Among these ideas was the topic of Systems Literacy introduced by Peter Tuddenham at the International Society for the Systems Sciences (ISSS) Annual Meeting in Berlin, Germany in August 2015. As team leaders developed their topics with their teams, they kept a focal theme of Systems Literacy in mind. The intention was that participants in the Conversation integrate the work of the teams into a body of knowledge to be developed into modes for educating those new to systems thinking, the systems sciences, and systems research, as a coordinated and coherent whole system initiative to define and achieve Systems Literacy.

Systems Literacy could be defined as understanding your model or models of Systems, how it is the same and different from others' models of Systems, and how our individual and collective actions influence Systems behaviors and how Systems behaviors influence us. An agreed definition will be an outcome of the Systems Literacy Initiative process.

The Systems Literacy Initiative is a process of an ongoing international, coordinated effort to create a greater awareness and understanding about "Systems" and to develop a comprehensive set of big ideas, supporting concepts and learning progressions that have broad agreement. At present, this Systems Literacy Initiative is now being developed by a working group of members from IFSR, ISSS, the International Council for Systems Engineers (INCOSE), and the American Society for Cybernetics (ASC).

At the 2016 IFSR Conversation welcome reception on Sunday evening, 3 April 2016, a brief introduction to the background, structure and process of other literacy efforts for the ocean, earth science, atmosphere, climate, and other subjects that can serve as models for Systems Literacy was presented by Peter Tuddenham. An invitation was extended to the participants to consider how their conversations during the week contribute to Systems Literacy in general, both content and process, and to engage for an hour at the end of each day to contribute to the content and participative design process for the Systems Literacy Initiative.

At the end of each day's conversations all teams assembled as one group to contribute to the Systems Literacy Initiative. On Monday the group answered the question "How would we know when we have a systems literate society?" Tuesday the group addressed issues of different representations of "Systems" in different languages and cultures. Another area of discussion was the Next Generation Science Standards in the USA that have cross-cutting concepts that are very close to a set of seven systems principles or considerations. The Wednesday contribution by the group was suggestions for other groups and parties who could be included in the broad Systems Literacy Initiative.

The IFSR 2016 Conversation overall theme of Systems Literacy was a helpful contribution to the overall multi organization Systems Literacy Initiative. Furthermore, the overall theme provided a way for some emergent properties of coherence and convergence to occur within each group's conversation.

Team 1: Exploring Transdisciplinarity using Hierarchy Theory, Boulding's Skeleton of Science, and General Systems Theory

Jennifer Wilby, Team Leader, United Kingdom - j.wilby@hull.ac.uk
Stefan Blachfellner, Austria - stefan.blachfellner@bcsss.org
Sue Gabriele, USA - sgabriele@gemslearning.net
Allenna Leonard, Canada - allenna_leonard@yahoo.com
Janet Singer, USA - jwillisinger@measures.org
Michael Singer, USA - mjsinger@soe.ucsc.edu

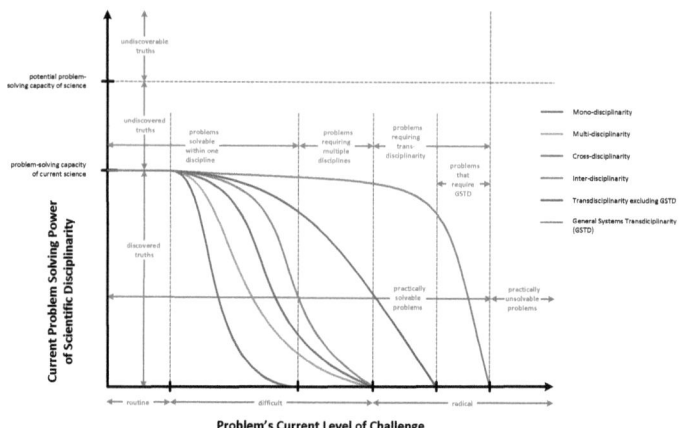

Figure 1. The application areas of kinds of disciplinarity (Rousseau, et al, 2016c)

The purpose of our Conversation at Linz was to discuss the hierarchy of systems complexity that Kenneth E. Boulding proposed in "General Systems Theory: The Skeleton of Science" (1956), drawing on his earlier work *The Image* (1956). We sought to explore the possibilities for informing a process of intentionally holistic transdisciplinarity. Members of this team have been involved with research that would feed into the transdisciplinarity conversation during the week-long meeting in Linz (Singer, et al. 2012; Rousseau et al, 2014, 2016 a,b,c). This work builds on von Bertalanffy's (1968) GST and the overarching unity, and Laszlo's (1972) systems philosophy as the underpinning unity. Throughout the week, we also discussed Sue Gabriele's framework for building relative Inclusive, Continuing, and Emancipatory (rICE) social systems starting from Boulding (1956), Checkland (1991), Scott (1992), and Gabriele (1997). Examples drew from her experience and research in schools and workplaces (see the conference proceedings for detailed discussion of this innovative framework).

Transdisciplinarity in practice requires more than simply bringing different disciplines into an intervention (Wilby, 2011a,b; Madni, 2007, 2010). Rousseau and Wilby (2014) argued that it will arise in practice from what could be called a General Systems Epistemology (GSE), and that development will be based on a radical change and design of practice coming from a unified single ontology. An initial ordering of increasing complexity in various forms of working in disciplinary practices, from mono-disciplinary practice towards the goal of transdisciplinary practice.

Figure 1 shows along the x-axis, the increasing level of challenge and increasing complexity in a problem situation, broken into 3 broad categories of routine, difficult, and radical. Known models and theories can be brought to bear on "routine" problems, but as the complexity increases, in a similar pattern displayed in Boulding's *Skeleton of Science*, then the theories and methods required to address "difficult" and "radical" problem situations are less certain in their application and outcomes.

In the current 2016 IFSR Conversation, the intent was to map specifically chosen systems methodologies in terms of Boulding's work, to demonstrate the systems principles incorporated (or not) in those methodologies, and where found, how those principles might be used to illuminate a possible form of a new transdisciplinarity in practice. What emerged from this week was a particular methodology (rICE), based on Boulding's *Skeleton of Science*, and how that may show transdisciplinarity in practice. An underlying theme in Kenneth Boulding's research and writing was the search for governing principles, rules and system structures. Boulding worked to discover some system of measurement (a form of gravimeter) applicable to the general field of social systems, similar to those found in the physical sciences. This was a framework that Scott referred to as a typology of system complexity (Scott, 1992). There are additional ways of viewing the Skeleton however, and it is these viewpoints on the content and context of Boulding's Skeleton we explored in our discussions.

Frameworks, clockworks, and control systems or "thermostats" (levels 1-3), are predictable, designable to exteriorly prescribed criteria (e.g., goals determined by a teacher, engineer, or CEO). Open, blueprint, image-aware, and symbol-processing parts (levels 4-7) are not designable. These undesignable systems, organisms, act according to interiorly prescribed criteria—needs (Level 4: e.g., ameba or living cell), abilities (Level 5: e.g., plant), perceptions (Level 6: e.g., animal), and choices (Level 7: human) -- of increasing variability. Level 4-7 system boundaries are mandatory. Level 8-9 system boundaries are fleeting, optional. Social and transcendent levels (Levels 8-9) are thus even more variable. Level 7 systems (humans) can ignore the leader's input and even take opposite action. Thus, Level 7 (individual) goals preempt Level 8 (organization) goals. Individual humans can move from one Level 8 system to another – changing their schools or workplaces. They cannot change their Level 7 system – their physical body.

Boulding's nine-level typology may clarify these two conflicting camps. In other words, top-down old paradigm bureaucratic models assume all parts of a social system are designable. New paradigm laissez-faire models assume no parts are designable. Boulding's typology shows how both paradigms are needed. The first step in the path to a more fully specified new paradigm for social system behavior is this shift in agency-- from teacher to learner, from CEO to employee. Whether behavioral laws and causes relate to gravity or human agency, both paradigm shifts here are proposed as hard science--a result of extensive empirical observation, rather than speculation. A shift at such a grand level requires reconceptualization and recalculation at all levels of system. Thus, development and applications are to be wide (across disciplines: cf. transdisciplinarity) and deep (at all levels of organization: cf. hierarchy theory).

Links to Hierarchy Theory and Transdisciplinarity

Gabriele's Figure 2 illustrates more specific areas for linking insights from Boulding's Typology to Hierarchy Theory and Transdisciplinarity. Left are examples of eight disciplines. There are the hard technical systems, where material agency dominates (Levels 1-3 in Boulding's Typology), and there are the soft social systems, where human agency dominates. Informed by transdisciplinarity, knowledge and concepts are to be meaningful, to make sense, across all the disciplines.

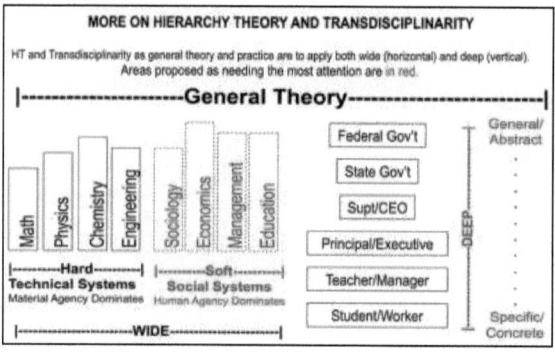

Figure 2. Illustrations of Hierarchy Theory and Transdisciplinarity

Far right is another dimension and continuum, from general and abstract to specific and concrete. Boulding affirmed that "Somewhere however between the specific that has no meaning and the general that has no content there must be, for each purpose and at each level of abstraction, an optimum degree of generality" (1956, 197). Thus, specific concepts and vocabulary are to be appropriately general or specific to be most meaningful at each level of organization and within each discipline.

Conclusions of the Conversation and Further Development of this Work

Given the complexity and scope of our topics, as well as our different images and viewpoints, there are many possibilities. We do anticipate further exploration and development of the core principles identified in Gabriele's elaboration of Boulding's typology, not yet developed during our work. We propose to explore them and link them to Hierarchy Theory and Transdisciplinarity in an intentionally holistic approach. Further conversation within the Team is ongoing to explore the relationships between Boulding's typology and the search for the evidence of transdisciplinary systemicity and some measurement of that concept in specific systems methodologies. Methodologies such as Soft Systems Methodology (SSM), the Viable System Model (VSM), System Dynamics (SD), and Complex Adaptive Systems (CAS) have yet to be evaluated for systemic principles incorporated (or not) in those methodologies, and where found, how those principles might be used to illuminate a new form of transdisciplinary practice, e.g. in Gabriele's rICE methodology.

Acknowledgements

The authors would like to thank Peter Tuddenham, Debora Hammond and David Rousseau for their thoughtful contributions to the team discussions during the week and in the writing of this report.

Team 1: Janet Singer, Allenna Leonard, guest contributor Peter Tuddenham, Sue Gabriele, Michael Singer, Stefan Blachfellner. (Team Leader Jennifer Wilby not pictured)

References

Boulding, K. E. (1956). General Systems Theory: The Skeleton of Science, *Management Science*, 2, 197-208.

Boulding, K. E. (1956). *The Image: Knowledge in Life and Society*, Ann Arbor Paperbacks, The University of Michigan Press.

Checkland, P. (1981). *Systems thinking, systems practice*. John Wiley and Sons, New York.

Gabriele, S. (1997). Boulding's typology elaborated: A framework for understanding school and classroom systems. *Systems Practice,* 10(3), 271–304.

Gabriele, S. (2014). *New Hope for Schools: Findings of a Teacher turned Detective*. iUniverse.

Laszlo E. (1972). *Introduction to Systems Philosophy: Toward a New Paradigm of Contemporary Thought*. Gordon & Breach, New York, NY.

Madni, A. M. (2007). Transdisciplinarity: Reaching beyond disciplines to find connections. *Journal of Integrated Design and Process Science*, *11*(1), 1-11.

Madni, A. M. (2010). Transdisciplinary system science: Implications for healthcare and other problems of global significance. *Transdisciplinary J Engineering Science*, *1*(1), 38-53.

Rousseau, D., & Wilby, J. M. (2014). Moving from Disciplinarity to Transdisciplinarity in the Service of Thrivable Systems. *Systems Research and Behavioral Science*, *31*(5), 666–677.

Rousseau, D., Wilby, J. M., Billingham, J., & Blachfellner, S. (2016a). A Typology for the Systems Field. *Systema*, *4*(1).

Rousseau, D., Wilby, J. M., Billingham, J., & Blachfellner, S. (2016b). Manifesto for General Systems Transdisciplinarity. *Systema*, *4*(1).

Rousseau, D., Wilby, J. M., Billingham, J., & Blachfellner, S. (2016c). The Scope and Range of General Systems Transdisciplinarity. *Systema*, *4*(1).

Scott, W. (1986). *Organizations: Rational, natural and open systems*. Prentice Hall, Englewood Cliffs, NJ.

Singer, J., Sillitto, H., Bendz, J., Chroust, G., Hybertson, D., Lawson, H.W., Martin, J., Martin, R., Singer, M., & Takaku, T. (2012). The Systems Praxis Framework, included in *Systems and Science at Crossroads – Sixteenth IFSR Conversation*, Linz, Austria.

Wilby, J. (2011). Essay: A new framework for viewing the philosophy, principles and practice of systems science. *Systems Research and Behavioral Science*, *28*(5), 437-442.

Wilby J, Macaulay L, & Theodoulidis B. (2011). Intentionally holistic knowledge intensive service systems, *International Journal of Services, Technology and Management* 16(2): 126–140.

Team 2: Unity in Diversity – Making the Implicit Explicit

Gary Smith, Co-Team Leader, United Kingdom - gary.smith@persescomms.com
Brigitte Daniel Allegro, Co-Team Leader, France - brigitte.daniel.allegro@gmail.com
Maria Stella Castro de Lobos, Brazil - clobo@hucff.ufrj.br
Gerhard Chroust, Austria - gerhard.chroust@jku.at
Florian Daniel, France - i.daniel.florian@gmail.com
Gordon Dyer, United Kingdom - gordon.dyer@btinternet.com
Xijin Tang, China - xjtang@iss.ac.cn

The origin for this conversation is that we put forth the case that it is in this time of crisis that we must break down the barriers to communication across disciplines, organizations, societies, beliefs and cultures in order to promote collective understanding for a common good.

Before the conversation, as a framework for communication we distributed the "Systems tree" which is a conceptual model of the "systems thinker's attitudes" and the key "systems concepts" that facilitate system understanding. The idea was explore these concepts, to develop a common understanding of their meaning and to have some experience in using them to consider different real world complex problems. This would allow us to develop a prototype game for teaching, exercising and developing systems thinking skills for all, which could be tuned to the diversity of potential players.

The journey started with the team a few weeks before the conversation itself in Linz: some e-mails were exchanged, some "exercises" done by the team, contributed papers were received to generate some ideas. We had a long video call with one member of the team and a short one with most of the other members.

Before the IFSR, we laid out a framework for the days in terms of team experience that we wanted to achieve:

- Sharing, playing and visualizing the system concepts
- Using the system concepts to analyze stories
- Building the framework for the game
- Using the game to analyze a real world problem

This was intended to facilitate the capture of the diversity of the team in the development of the toolbox for the prototype game.

Our first meeting with the team did not go so well. One of the team members did not want to review the objectives for why we were there and to engage in a conversation on the way forward. After what seemed to be an impasse, one team member suggested to use a story called "The Baron and Baroness" as a way to exercise systems thinking. This we did and it promoted a better atmosphere for conversation and to get to know each other a little better.

After the story and lunch, we all produced some drawings of concepts which helped a little in sharing the idea that we can express concepts not just in words but also through art. For example when we played with the concept of boundary there were several different representations which highlighted different features of personal perspective.

One day two, we started with a systems thinking roundtable. This gave the opportunity for everyone to speak and to express what were their hopes and expectations for the conversation. The questions asked were: "What is Systems thinking? What are the challenges and what are your hopes? What situations have your left behind and what might happen here that could be valuable for you back home?"

During the second day we shared some more stories and we also took the time to explore the Chinese characters related to system concepts. By the end of this day, we had agreed what the nature of the game would be in terms of qualities and framework. Its scalability and the idea that it's scaling and tailoring could be made using the concepts in relationship to the stories and games already embedded in culture.

On the third day we were joined by one of the other team leaders who ran a round table on the topic of "what can you do to support systems literacy". We also then reran the Baron and Baroness Story but this time as observers.

We then started to fill in a matrix of system concepts and related simple questions that could be asked in relationship to simple stories. We used an Aesop tale – "the cock and the jewel". We focused here on questions that could be asked to young children of age 3-5. What we realized is that dependent on the level of systems experience we could speak the language and use questions tailored to the level of the player. What we also realized was that some concepts were more applicable to simple situations, whilst others were more attributable to complex situations.

Gary, Brigitte planning the game

On the fourth day we started again with another round table on the topic of "Unity in Diversity". We finished a document that described the overview of the game, incorporating the Baron/Baroness story as the example. The team came up with the idea to produce a digital platform for capturing system concepts, related information such as visualization and questions. These questions where designed and related through simple, complicated, complex and "wicked" situations. The team worked very quickly in the afternoon to define digital cards and questions for many of the system concepts. Everyone was able to work within the proposed framework and make very strong contributions. In the evening we finished off the presentation for the next day.

Through the experience we have made some adaptions to the original systems tree framework. Some concepts were renamed and some others were added.

In the end we had accomplished pretty much what we aimed at, but the experience was much more difficult than expected. Also the prototype game was different to what we were expecting, digital instead of a tangible art. This proved to be enabler for development in an adaptable, collaborative way, thus providing a better framework for teaching, developing and practicing "Systemry" that would be scalable and adaptable to all possible users and cultures.

Reflecting on the overall experience, the most compelling aspects of the team's conversation is that can be very difficult to lead a team on a journey without having first developed a common vision and mission. In fact the first journey we had to make was the discovery of each other and our plan to build the team was dismissed at the start. As a consequence several members of the team on the first day became observers rather than full participants. On a much more positive note, after the first day each of the team members were invited and able to share and suggest insightful contributions.

After the conversation, for the game itself, "SysteMystery" as a platform is in development based on the matrix developed at IFSR. Once initially tested, it will be opened for the team to contribute to its enrichment. It is hoped that this

framework might be a useful contribution to the systems literacy project.

The Unity in Diversity Team

Team 2: Gordon Dyer, Maria Stella de Castro Lobo, Florian Daniel, Gary Smith (Co-Team Leader), Brigitte Daniel Allegro (Co-Team Leader), Xijin Tang, and Gerhard Chroust (not pictured)

Team 3: Systems Research Team - Exploring the Relationship of Systems Research to Systems Literacy

> Mary Edson, Team Leader, USA – maredson.s3@gmail.com
> Pam Buckle Henning, USA – buckle@adelphi.edu
> Tim Ferris, United Kingdom - timothy.ferris@cranfield.ac.uk
> Andreas Hieronymi, Switzerland- – andreas.hieronymi@unisg.ch
> Ray Ison, United Kingdom – ray.ison@open.ac.uk
> Gary Metcalf, USA – gmetcalf@interconnectionsllc.com
> George Mobus, USA – gmobus@uw.edu
> Nam Nguyen, Australia - nam.nguyen@mzsg.com
> David Rousseau - david.rousseau@systemsphilosophy.org
> Shankar Sankaran, Australia - shankar.sankaran@uts.edu.au
> Peter Tuddenham - peter@coexploration.net (guest member)

This summary outlines the activities and outcomes of the Systems Research Team (SRT) at the 2016 IFSR Conversation in Linz, Austria. While the 2014 SRT focused on the needs of Systems Researchers, the 2016 SRT's focus is on reaching out to a broader community to provide a foundation for Systems Literacy. The team's Conversation revolved around the question,

"How can Systems Research be in service to Systems Literacy?" The team's discussions were directed into two essential aspects, separate and integrated, of this question. First, Systems Research serves Systems Literacy by providing a credible foundation for the principles and practices of Systems Science and Systems Thinking in both systematic and systemic modes. Second, Systems Research provides a neutral frame for development of ethical applications of those principles and practices.

The SRT recognizes the exigency in providing foundational principles that can be effectively adopted and disseminated through Systems Literacy. The team's narrative begins with an understanding the urgency for application of Systems Sciences and Systems Thinking to critical issues. Systems research is typically a slow generation of results; however, the body of knowledge gained through this process can be confidently used to address complexity in timely ways. The choice of how we respond to these issues relates to a process model that can be applied. Through understanding the relationship of the process model to the trajectory, the team directed its focus to developing a MindMap of eight essential aspects or features of how Systems Research can support Systems Literacy. These include: Systems Science knowledge base, roles and personas, maturity models, role profile, ontology/vocabulary, perspective/framing choice, frameworks, and political ecology. The eight relate to unpacking the Systems landscape in a coherent but loosely coupled investment portfolio (economic, social, and relational) for building *systemic sensibility* in such a way as to be dis/aggregated for different audiences. The week's work culminated in a plan for "Looking Ahead," which outlines the intentions of the SRT to continue to its activities in support of Systems Literacy in the upcoming months. The following sections summarize the SRT's Conversation.

Exigency of Systems Research to Systems Literacy

The necessity for Systems approaches to address larger issues and problems informed much of the Conversation, as the limitations of traditional approaches have been realized. Economies and societies are going through a Great Transformation. While in earlier times, societal revolutions were induced by technological innovations, today social technology of system-cybernetic management will revolutionize the functioning of companies, societal organisations and whole countries (Malik, 2016). For us, as an individual systems scientists/scholars and also, collectively, as the systems society, it is critical to find ways to move ourselves and the systems field, together with systems research and systems literacy.

Process Model

In this vein, we asked ourselves, "Why do we care about systems science, systems literacy and systems approaches?" The purpose is not just about increasing the amount of systems books and papers, but finally about the changes we want to see in the world. How can we bridge the perceived gap between academic knowledge and real-world practice? What are the necessary intermediary factors from insight to impact? The following process model (Figure 1) tries to capture this and consists of five main variables/factors (or pillars) that are linked through a sixth one.

Systems Analysis – Future Potentials

The process started here, at the Conversation, which is essentially an agile method for finding a set of seed ideas. The Conversation has provided an excellent beginning for a more rigorous top-down systems analysis. Here is a sense of what the SRT is working on and toward.

The SRT is *acting as a process to generate a process*, i.e. to develop a framework for the production of a set of guiding principles, including possible structures to be employed, for the doing of systems research. The intent of this effort is that by doing so future systems researchers (in different roles such as pure or applied research) will contribute to a common framework in which the other sciences (natural and social alike) can operate to enhance and increase the systemicity of their work. The objective includes a broader application of systems literacy that goes beyond just doing science to the whole of social thinking and doing. The work started here must eventually be witnessed succeeding as social norms in thinking through complex problems (e.g. political) and move from linear, isolated conceptualization to the systems point of view.

To that end the team identified eight believably critical factors or components that form the structural aspects of the hoped for process. George proposed the application of a kind of systems analysis (Mobus, 2015) to what we have so far in order to better identify the actual processes that will produce the actual products and resource inputs needed. Through an iterative process of feedback exchanged with the team, the SRT in essence becomes the "users" (actors or agents) thus capturing the real needs of the users. In other words, the members of the SRT are not merely attempting to be objective observers of processes but participants in the systems in which they research, possibly as agents of change and transformation.

Eight Critical Factors

After identifying eight, believably critical factors or components that form the structural aspects of the hoped for process our team decided to explore these further. As shown in the Process Model, the list of eight factors we compiled are:

1.) Systems Body of Knowledge,
2.) Systems Personas,
3.) Systems Maturity Models,
4.) Systems Role/Profile,
5.) Systems Ontology/Vocabulary,
6.) Systems Perspective/Framing Choice,
7.) Systems Frameworks, and
8.) Systems Political Ecology.

Starting with Systems Body of Knowledge, these eight factors were unpacked.

Knowledge Base of a Discipline

A generic way of modelling the structure of the knowledge base of a discipline is suitable for the SRT's purpose. This model was developed by the General Systems Transdisciplinarity team (Rousseau et al., 2016). Three important things should be noted at the outset.

First, the building up of the knowledge base depends on factors that are not part of the knowledge base per se but originate in the discipline's guidance framework. This includes the definition of the subject of interest for the discipline (creating an empirical boundary for the discipline) and a technical vocabulary (which, like the empirical boundary, can be interpreted differentially based on worldviews of individual scientists). Second, the basic knowledge base model is very simple, making the model easy to apply. It shows that the knowledge base consists of data, three kinds of theories and also methodologies (with all these terms very broadly construed). This provides a framework for elaboration as shown in Figure 2.

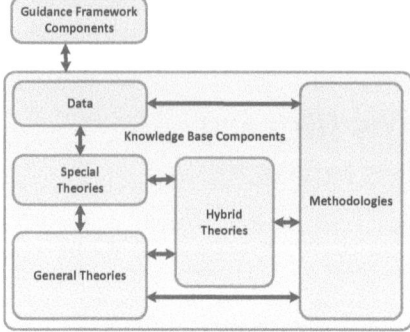

Figure 2. The structure of a Knowledge Base (adapted from Rousseau et al., 2016, Fig. 9)

Third, the knowledge base of any discipline is typically developed by working through a set of structured questions about the disciplinary subject, namely what are the subject entities like, how do they work, how do they come about, and why some types and design not appear or persist. At each stage we develop descriptions and theories that can support the development of methodologies. The questions address increasingly systemic issues - complexity ("what are entities like?"), machine models ("how does it work?"), developmental and evolutionary mode (how do they come about?) and eventually holistic models ("why do only some types appear or persist?). This kind of model can therefore be useful in the context of several of the components of the "investment portfolio' the SRT discussed as a framework for guiding activities that would make progress towards achieving systemic literacy and sensibility in the broader community.

Systems Landscape and Systemic Sensibilities

Ray urged the team to frame the next steps of the contribution of the SRT (or rebranded as the 'Landscape of Systems Knowing Inquiry') as we devised a 'first-cut' model (Figure 1) of an 'investment portfolio' as a device to aid on-going inquiry by us, as well as a means to organize and report on our work and that of other groups committed to supporting transitions to systemic literacy (systemic sensibility + [systems science + systems thinking in practice or STiP]) (Blackmore, C., Reynolds, M., Ison, R. & Lane, A., 2015).

We understand investment to include financial, individual, intellectual, group, organizational, philanthropic, among other characteristics or attributes, and the 'portfolio' to be designed drawing on concepts of self-organization, open-source protocols, and easy refinement for different purposes/investors. We suggest that in a 'first-cut' portfolio design each of the eight elements needs to utilize/complete the following template:

What is the element - characterize it?
Why is it important?
What is a story (narrative) or case study about it - of need, failure, success, etc.?
Suggest possible 'investment' agendas or pathways - who; how; when?

Perhaps this template needs to be completed also for the outer 'system' in Figure 2 - hence the question mark? Monitoring and evaluation systems against agreed, yet adaptable, measures of performance are needed 'in service' of moving towards systemic literacy. Controlling action will also be needed. These 'systems' will also require a conducive institutional/organizational platform from which to operate and thrive.

Shadow Side of Systems - Systems Ethics

Systems Literacy could benefit from looking at the ethics of Systems Research and in Systems Practice and some of its nascent assumptions. There is general agreement among scholars and practitioners interested in systems science and systemic methods that using systemic perspectives will enable them to produce better results in their work than they would achieve if they were to continue to use the discipline perspective approaches to their work that traditionally would have been applied. The improvement that they perceive achieving through the use of systemic perspectives results from producing results reflecting a more complete vision of the situation which enables more complete understanding of the interaction between the aspects of the situation and reducing unintended consequences, and the knowledge to deal with the emergent effects more effectively through better understanding of what they reflect about the situation. This aspect of improvement in work approached systemically improves the results achieved, so the word "good" is appropriate to reflect that the results of work done systemically are more likely to match the actor's intent. That is, these results are "good" from the perspective of the actor intervening in the situation.

As a result systems research and practice must be understood as morally neutral, with potential to be used for good or ill, and therefore in developing systems knowledge, or in the rhetoric of discussing systems and systemic approaches to engagement with the world, it is necessary to avoid the assumption of moral desirability of systemic perspectives, and also to discuss systemic approaches in a way that recognizes where the moral judgement of the systems practitioner or researcher will impact the choices made.

Looking Ahead and Moving Forward

The SRT left the 2016 Conversation in Linz with two commitments and an invitation. A valuable framework (i.e. the "investment portfolio") had been created, but needed to be further refined and explored. The first commitment was for a team discussion in June, after time for additional reflection, which has taken place. The second commitment was preparation of a presentation for the ISSS 2016 Conference in Boulder, CO. An invitation is for others, beyond the team, who find the initial work to be interesting enough to help in its further development. The true value of the portfolio will be demonstrated by the additional investment that it draws.

Conclusions and Recommendations

The SRT's Conversation focused on the question, "How can Systems Research be in service to Systems Literacy?" To reiterate, discussions were coalesced into two essential aspects. First, Systems Research serves Systems Literacy by providing a credible foundation for the principles and practices of Systems Science and Systems Thinking in both systematic and systemic ways. Second, Systems Research provides an impartial, dispassionate frame for development of ethical applications of those principles and practices.

In the team's view, successful programs in Systems Literacy will be grounded in Systems Research encompassing: 1.) a *history* of systems thinking (context, sources, and development of key ideas – principles expressed in clear language); 2.) *literature* of systems (a canon of essential theory, results of practice, and criticism); and 3) *transdisciplinarity* (shared relations and effects of systems sciences with other disciplines). The SRT's role is to foster the relationship between these aspects of Systems Research with Systems Literacy in timely and relevant ways.

Team 3: (L to R) Nam Nguyen, Ray Ison, David Rousseau, George Mobus, Mary Edson, Tim

Ferris, Shankar Sankaran, Gary Metcalf, Pam Buckle Henning, Andreas Hieronymi, and Peter Tuddenham (not pictured)

References:

Blackmore, C., Reynolds, M., Ison, R. & Lane, A. (2015). Embedding sustainability through systems thinking in practice: some experiences from the Open University. In: Wyness, Lynne ed. *Education for Sustainable Development Pedagogy: Criticality, Creativity, and Collaboration.* PedRIO occasional papers (8). Plymouth University:

Pedagogic Research Institute and Observatory (PedRIO), 32–35.

Malik, F. (2016). *Navigating Into The Unknown. A New Way for Management, Governance and Leadership*. Campus: Frankfurt am Main/New York.

Mobus, G. E., & Kalton, M. C. (2015). *Principles of systems science*. New York, NY: Springer.

Rousseau, D., Billingham, J., Wilby, J. M., & Blachfellner, S. (2016). In Search of General Systems Theory. *Systema*, 4(1). [forthcoming]

List of Participants of the Conversation

Participants	Country	Team *
Brigitte Daniel Allegro	FR	2
Stefan Blachfellner	AT	1
Gerhard Chroust	AT	2
Florian Daniel	FR	2
Gordon Dyer	UK	2
Mary Edson	US	3
Tim Ferris	UK	3
Sue Gabriel	US	1
Andreas Hieronymi	CH	3
Pam Henning	US	3
Ray Ison	UK	3
Allenna Leonard	CDN	1
Maria Stella Castro-Lobo	BR	2
Gary Metcalf	US	3
George Mobus	US	3
Nam Nguyen	AU	3
David Rousseau	UK	3
Gary Smith	US	2
Janet Willis Singer	USA	1
Michael Singer	USA	1
Shankar Sankaran	AU	3
Xijin Tang	CN	2
Peter Tuddenham	US	3
Jennifer Wilby	UK	1

*) Team 1: Exploring Transdisciplinarity using Hierarchy Theory,

Team 2: Unity In Diversity – make the implicit explicit

Team 3: Systems Research: A Foundation for Systems Literacy

Systems Literacy

(Peter Tuddenham)

In April 2016, the IFSR Conversation had chosen the theme Systems Literacy. Here I will describe how this theme came to be and provide background information on similar efforts in the ocean sciences, earth sciences, atmospheric sciences, and other related disciplines. This is also a personal reflection on a systems journey that began for me in 1979 in the United Kingdom and continued when I moved to the USA in 1980.

IFSR has on its website at the top the slogan "Uniting the world in Systems Science". And the IFSR website http://www.ifsr.org displays this statement: "The overall purpose of the Federation is to advance cybernetic and systems research and systems applications in order to serve the international systems community ". (What is the IFSR?, 2016) Many, if not all, of us reading this will have varying degrees of commitment to this purpose, and will be pursuing it as best we can. The IFSR has 45 member organizations around the world. The total number of people represented by these organizations is hard to determine, but I expect that the international systems community is in the thousands. Uniting the world and advancing systems and cybernetic ideas then is a major undertaking to unite the world in systems science with a population of nearly 7,500,000,000 at the end of 2016. (World Population 2016)

Moreover, attempting to unite the systems community is an ongoing challenge. Charles Francois produced the International Encyclopedia of Systems and Cybernetics in 1997 (Francois 1997) which has over 20 columns devoted to the definition of system. Similarly, Dr. Eric Shwarz mapped "Some Streams of Systemic Thought". He color coded twelve streams of historic development: general systems, cybernetics, physical sciences, mathematics, computers and informatics, biology and medicine, symbolic systems, social systems, ecology, philosophy, systems analysis, and engineering. The vast number of contributions to these systemic thought streams presents a complex set of relationships and dependencies. A large map demonstrates the density and complexity of the field and can be seen at http://www.cybertech-engineering.ch/index.php/en/blog-de/research-development/item/14-some-streams-of-systemic-thought

There are many authors of books and journal articles who are contributing to ways that bring varying degrees of clarity to this diversity and complexity in various ways. They come from a variety of perspectives, philosophy, science perspective originating in biological sciences, or cognitive and learning science to systems engineering to systems software programming, to name just a few. Rousseau et al. (Rousseau 2016) is on a "Search for General Systems Theory" towards what he calls GST* which is an overarching encompassing philosophical work of the transdisciplinary nature of systems. Troncale (Troncale 2013) offers Systems Processes and Pathologies: Creating an Integrated Framework for Systems Science, which is a culmination of a career researching and teaching systems. Cabrera et al. (Cabrera 2008) have identified four fundamental patterns that connect the system universe: Distinctions, Systems, Relationships, and Perspective. Specific communities are also pursuing ways to clarify systems sciences for their applications. Martin and Ferris have summarized systems as it impacts the practice of systems engineering. (Martin 2008) Another compilation of system sciences is described by Mobus and Kalton in their book "Principles of Systems Sciences" (Mobus 2015) in which they list 12 Systems Science Principles. Esbjorn-Hargans and Zimmerman (Esbjorn-Hargens 2009) describe an "Integral Ecology: Uniting Multiple Perspectives on the Natural World. Cajete (Cajete 2000) articulates the view of Native Thinking towards all systems, with an Indigenous view of reality, examining natural forces and all forms of life. Fritjof Capra and Pier Luigi in "The Systems View of Life" show how over the past 30 years "a new systemic conception of life has emerged at the forefront of science." (Capra 2014).

The Millennium Project identifies 15 Global Challenges. (Glenn 2015) The top 3 are: 1. How can sustainable development be achieved for all while addressing global climate change? 2. How can everyone have sufficient clean water without conflict? and 3. How can population growth and resources be brought into balance? Many responses to these 15 challenges are from the systems community, for example Ray Ison (Ison 2010) suggests ways to act using systems practice in a climate-change world while Angela Espinosa and Jon Walker (Espinoza 2011) give practical examples of cybernetic models used to understand and manage eco systems in their book "A Complexity Approach to Sustainability". The ideas and approaches exist in so many ways, yet most students and adults do not know they exist let alone have ways to apply the rich possibilities of approaches, management, and sustainable practices to their lives.

From some of my earliest days in junior and high school in North London, England in the 1960's and early 1970's I have wondered why the teaching was delivered in 45-60 minute segments in what I came to know in the USA as stove-piped subjects. On many occasions, I was frustrated by the reaction of teachers to the question of how one subject related to another subject. I was told to concentrate on the specific discipline. I sought ways to find connections. I did find some help by taking an A Level called Physical Science. This was an innovative attempt by the Nuffield Foundation (Nuffield Foundation 1973) to produce an attempt at a curriculum change that was a largely conceptual course of study that dealt with the structure and properties of matter at the borders of physics and chemistry. I wonder if that was an introduction for me to the questions of boundary determination and perspectives? After school I joined the British Army Corps of Royal Engineers as a 2nd Lieutenant, where the beginning of the motto is "Ubique" in English "Everywhere", a beginning for me of a quest to make connections.

My first introduction to the language and field of systems was in 1978 in Unit One on the first page of an Open University course in the United Kingdom called Approaches to Industrial Relations. (Beishon 1976) The authors of the first course reader, Brian Barrett and John Beishon, described the importance of defining "problem areas" knowing the who, why and where of boundary drawing, the description of the environment, the role of the observer, and distinctions about unitary and pluralist frameworks. Before proceeding with the content of the Industrial Relations course a whole section was devoted to "Systems and Systems Approaches" with a focus on using systems terms and concepts to describe systems behaviors. I was intrigued and excited by this approach. The following year I enrolled in a second Open University course called Systems Behaviour. (Peters 1977) This course presented case studies of activities in nature and society and human relations and then offered different systems approaches to describe, define, model and build simulations of them. This course is no longer offered.

Furthermore, the Systems Department at the United Kingdom's Open University is no longer a separate department and is now a group that is a part of the Faculty of Computing Mathematics and Technology. Over the 35-year history the systems group has reached more than 30, 000 people. (SysWeb - The Open University of Systems Group Website 2016).

At the very time all sectors of society could be benefiting from cybernetic and systems research and systems applications there seems to be a diminishing appreciation of the depth and breadth of the possibilities.

I rejoined the systems and cybernetic academic community at the joint International Society for Systems Sciences (ISSS) conference and American Cybernetic Society in Washington D.C. in 2014 and then again in Berlin in 2015 (International Society for Systems Sciences Annual Conference Berlin 2015). There I found numerous systems and cybernetic voices seeking primacy. Many of the attendees at the ISSS conference were also members of IFSR and the International Council of Systems Engineers (INCOSE). I have also been a member of the American Society for Cybernetics. All of these systems community organizations and their members are producing a cacophony of systems and cybernetic ideas, messages, theories, practices and methodologies.

However, while in Berlin I began to share my experience over the past 15 years with the geoscience education, science, and policy community in the USA. The lack of clarity in the systems and cybernetic communication situation is not dissimilar to the one I encountered in the ocean science community in the USA in 2002 and the Earth science community in 2009. There was a level of frustration in the ocean science, ocean education and ocean policy communities that no, or very little, education on the ocean and its role in the planet and our lives was a part of any school curriculum.

Think about your own education, did you learn much or anything about the sea and ocean? The ocean covers over 70% of the planet surface, is a major influence on weather and climate, has significant influences on our food, security, economic, social, spiritual, scientific, artistic, transportation and recreational lives and experiences, yet is virtually unknown.

Yet we started a project in 2004 to resolve the lack of ocean education and lack of agreement about what ocean science topics should be taught, or could be used to teach science, in schools in the USA. An ocean literacy initiative was launched to bring together scientists, educators, and policy makers in a process to define ocean literacy, to identify and describe seven fundamental principles and supporting concepts. I was one of four people on a small committee that organized a participative and representative process over a year long period that resulted in a definition, principles and concepts of ocean literacy and the production of a guide, as well as a strong collaborative community of practice that continues in various ways 15 years later. (Ocean Literacy 2016)

During the ISSS 2015 Annual Conference the suggestion to create a Systems Literacy initiative similar in process, structure and promotion to the Ocean Literacy and Earth Science work was generally agreed. The current president of IFSR, Mary Edson, suggested that Systems Literacy might be considered as an integrating theme for the IFSR 2016 conversations in Linz, Austria.

Therefore, as the theme for the 2016 conversations of the IFSR in Linz, Austria was Systems Literacy (IFSR CONVERSATION 2016 (April 2 – 8, Linz, Austria), 2016). I hope we can see growing interest in developing a Systems Literacy initiative that ensures that the top 7-9 big ideas, or principles and their supporting concepts from the significant body of work related to the systems field, from systems sciences to cybernetics are taught in schools and understood and applied in society.

The U.S. National Science Foundation and U.S. Geological Service asked the College of Exploration to support a similar effort to develop an Earth Science Literacy guide. (Wysession 2012) This provided to be more challenging in many ways as Earth Science was already an established topic taught in schools, yet the Earth Science community had never come together to collectively decide the big ideas and supporting concepts. More details on the process and results are at http://www.earthscienceliteracy.org

The model of ocean literacy and earth science literacy (Geosciences Literacy 2008), along with climate and atmosphere literacy initiatives are models and patterns to consider and use as we develop an integrated, participative, and as inclusive as possible, Systems Literacy initiative. To ground a Systems Literacy effort in natural systems not only grounds the effort literary but also allows for emergence based on real experience. Other related efforts include Ecological Literacy or Ecoliteracy (Stone 2005) and Environmental Literacy (Environmental Literacy 2016) There are many other literacy efforts that can be reviewed, a number are summarized on the College of Exploration website at http://www.coexploration.org/literacy

The word literacy is not without its difficulties. The concept is not easily translated into some languages. From 2002-2012 UNESCO sponsored a decade of literacy. (Literacy Decade 2012) and has significant resources on literacy on its website. For many the concept of literacy implies reading and writing. However, a broader definition is described in Chapter Six of the UNESCO Education for All Global Monitoring Report (Education for All Global Monitoring

Report 2006) . The U.S. National Academies of Science have recently described Science Literacy in a report thus: *"Science is a way of knowing about the world. At once a process, a product, and an institution, science enables people to both engage in the construction of new knowledge as well as use information to achieve desired ends. Access to science—whether using knowledge or creating it—necessitates some level of familiarity with the enterprise and practice of science: we refer to this as science literacy."* (Dibner 2016)

The Ocean Literacy initiative in the USA is designed to use ocean science content to enable teachers to meet science education objectives and standards. To achieve agreement from the different ocean disciplines was the first task. Each different discipline in the ocean sciences had its priorities. A consensus was required from the such disciplines as Physical, Biological, Chemical, Geography, Meteography and Geology Oceanographers. The process of reaching this consensus along with a report on the outputs and outcomes is in the report "Science Content and Standards for Ocean Literacy: An Ocean Literacy Update" published in 2005 (Cava 2005).

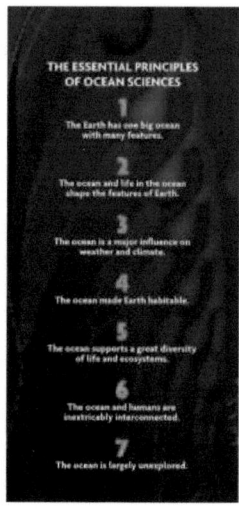

THE ESSENTIAL PRINCIPLES
OF SYSTEMS (SCIENCES)
1
One .. Whole
2
Shape..form..model..
3
Major influence on...
4
Systems make our life.. Patterns..Flows.. Cycles
5
Systems are diverse..
6
Systems ...humans
7.
More to learn, explore, understand

Figure 1 Using Ocean Literacy Principles as a Pattern for Systems Literacy

Three of the significant outputs of the Ocean Literacy initiative are the guide, a scope and sequence for K-12 education and a website http://www.oceanliteracy.net. The guide has a page with the 7 principles that could be used as a starting discussion for 7 principles of systems and cybernetic literacy. A suggestion is in Figure 1. The ocean principles are then supported with over 45 concepts. This work was then supported by a set of learning progressions of over 700 learning elements contained in diagrams for each of four separate grade bands. The whole set is on the Ocean Literacy website, an example from Principle 1 Kindergarten to Grade 2 (K-2) (ages 5 to 8 years) is shown in Figure 2. As the ages and grades increase the maps or scope and sequence learning progressions become more complex and are therefore better viewed online at the ocean literacy website. The density of the nodes do not reproduce well in a written paper such as this one.

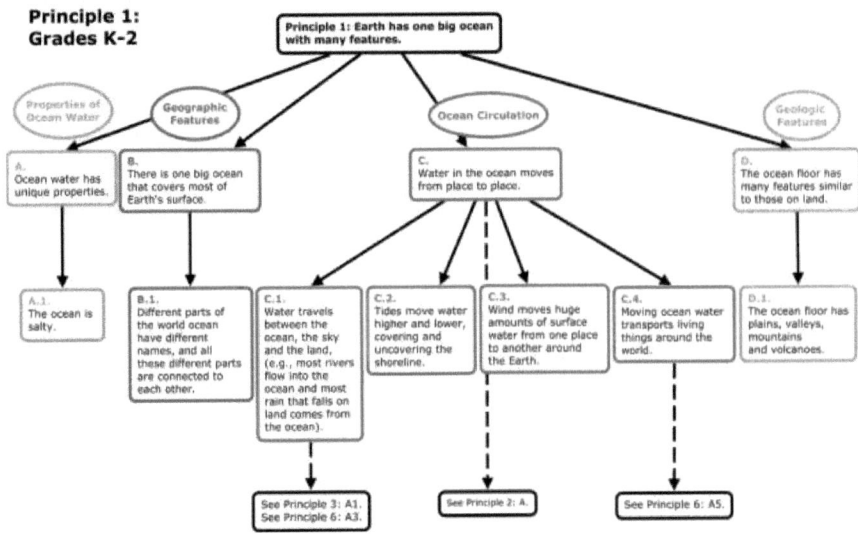

Figure 2 Scope and Sequence for Ocean Literacy Principle 1, Grades K-2

Since the publication of the first guide in 2005 the US Ocean Literacy initiative has influenced many actions around the world. The Smithsonian Sant Ocean hall used the 7 principles to guide its programming; European Union, Canada and the United States signed the Galway Agreement on Atlantic Ocean Cooperation and agreed to promote ocean literacy (Atlantic Programme Signed 2013); and most recently the European Union's Horizon 2020 funding has committed 6 million Euros to two projects to promote ocean literacy in Europe (Horizon 2020 Ocean Literacy 2015).

The term Systems Literacy has been used before. Fred Crowell proposed "Systems Literacy and the Literate Design of Educational Systems" at the 36th Annual Meeting of the International Society for Systems Sciences. He examined Systems Literacy as a design concept. His description of Systems Literacy was based on a definition of systems as a way to look at the world, so "then Systems Literacy would seem to indicate the capability of knowing and communicating about ways of looking at the world." (Crowell 1992) The term Systems Literacy is used by the Public Broadcasting Service at http://www.pbslearningmedia.org/collection/systemsliteracy/ based in large part on systems dynamics. These are both important contribution to the effort proposed here. However, what I would like to see is a far more all-encompassing initiative.

Another encouraging and supporting document is the Appendix G, Cross Cutting Concepts of the Next Generation Science Standards of the USA. (Achieve Inc 2013) These are 7 concepts that have been described in previous work as "Unifying Concepts". Including and developing them as part of Systems Literacy initiative is recommended. The 7 concepts are:

1. *Patterns.* Observed patterns of forms and events guide organization and classification, and they prompt questions about relationships and the factors that influence them.

2. *Cause and effect: Mechanism and explanation.* Events have causes, sometimes simple, sometimes multifaceted. A major activity of science is investigating and explaining causal relationships and the mechanisms by which they are mediated. Such mechanisms can then be tested across given contexts and used to predict and explain events in new contexts.

3. *Scale, proportion, and quantity.* In considering phenomena, it is critical to recognize what is relevant at different measures of size, time, and energy and to recognize how changes in scale, proportion, or quantity affect a system's structure or performance.

4. *Systems and system models.* Defining the system under study—specifying its boundaries and making explicit a model of that system—provides tools for understanding and testing ideas that are applicable throughout science and engineering.

5. *Energy and matter: Flows, cycles, and conservation.* Tracking fluxes of energy and matter into, out of, and within systems helps one understand the systems' possibilities and limitations.

6. *Structure and function.* The way in which an object or living thing is shaped and its substructure determine many of its properties and functions.

7. *Stability and change.* For natural and built systems alike, conditions of stability and determinants of rates of change or evolution of a system are critical elements of study.

Figure 3 The 7 Unifying Concepts from the U.S. Next Generation Science Standards, Appendix G

As the liaison between the ISSS and INCOSE, Janet Singer suggested that the proposed Systems Literacy initiative could be helpful in the work of the Systems Sciences Working Group of INCOSE. (Systems Science Working Group 2016). A half day workshop on the topic was planned for the INCOSE International Workshop in California in January 2016. (P. S. Tuddenham 2016) Later in the year the INCOSE International Symposium a full day workshop on Systems Literacy was organized (P. Tuddenham 2016).

The systems engineering community has a growing interest in the theoretical foundations of systems engineering. Systems science is one significant field that is of interest, and consequently this Systems Literacy effort has the potential to make a significant contribution. One approach to diagramming complex systems developed by Boardman and Sauser (Boardman 2013). In December 2015 I used their approach and software to create a "systemigram" of the developing ideas for Systems Literacy (Figure 4).

This needs to be updated now after the 2016 IFSR Conversation and other developments.

Developing a comprehensive, yet succinct, guide for Systems Literacy is a bold and audacious goal. However, with the experience of the geoscience literacy work I have contributed to I think it is achievable. Following the IFSR Conversations in 2016 two keynotes on Systems Literacy were presented at the 60th Annual Conference of the International Society for Systems Sciences and a whole day workshop on Systems Literacy completed at the 2016 INCOSE International Symposium in Edinburgh. Further activities are publications are being planned by IFSR, ISSS and INCOSE for 2017. I believe that in an increasingly rapidly changing, interdependent and technologically driven world we have a duty to bring more awareness and application of the richness of the field of systems and cybernetics to all sectors of society. To achieve that we need a systems literate society.

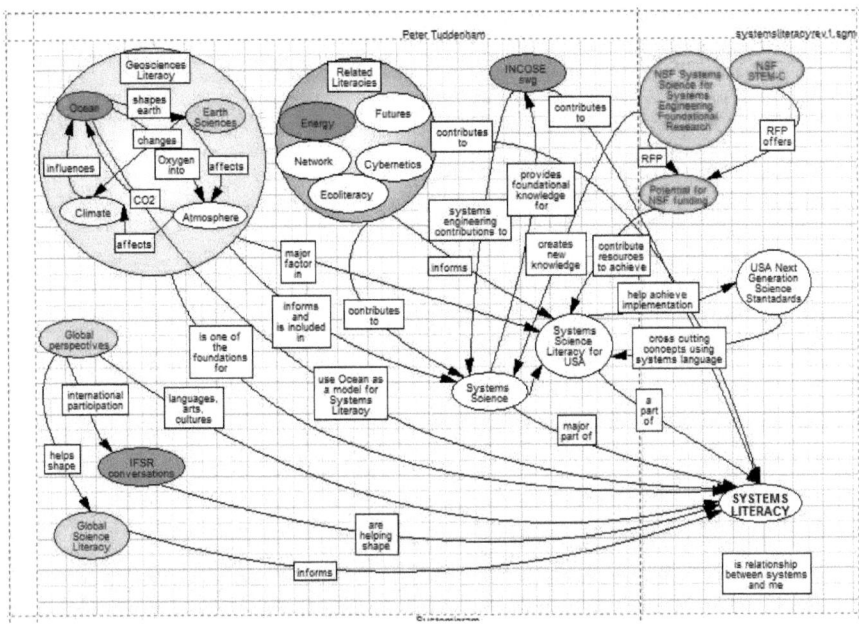

Figure 4 Systemigram of Ocean Literacy created in December 2015

References:

Achieve Inc. 2013. *Next Generation Science Standards, For States, By States, Volume 2 Appendixes.* Washington D.C.: The National Academies Press.

2013. *Atlantic Programme Signed.* http://atlanticoceanliteracy.wp2.coexploration.org/files/2013/07/Atlantic-Programme-Signed.pdf.

Beishon, John, and Brian Barrett. 1976. *Unit 1: Approaches to Industrial Relations.* Milton Keynes: The Open University.

Boardman, John and Brian Sauser. 2013. *Systemic Thinking: Building Maps for Worlds of Systems.* Hoboken: John Wiley and Sons Inc.

Cabrera, D., Colosi, L., Lobdell, c. 2008. "Systems Thinking." *Evaluation and Program Planning* 299-310.

Cajete, Gregory.,. 2000. *Native Science: Natural Laws of Interdependence.* Santa Fe: Clear Light Publishers.

Capra, Fritjof, and Luisi, Pier Luigi. 2014. *A Systems View of Life: A Unifying Vision.* Cambridge: Cambridge University Press.

Cava, F., Schoedinger, S., Strang, C., Tuddenham.P. 2005. *Science Content and Standards for Ocean Literacy: An Ocean Literacy Update* . Potomac Falls: College of Exploration. http://www.coexploration.org/oceanliteracy/documents/OLit2004_Final_000.pdf.

Crowell, Fred A. 1992. "Systems Literacy and the Literate Design of Educational Systems." *General Systems Approaches to Alternative Economics and Values: Proceedings of the 36th Annual Meeting of the International Society.* Denver: The Society. 964-975.

Dibner, Catherine E. Snow and Kenne A. 2016. *Science Literacy: Concepts, Contexts, and Consequences.* Washington D.C.: National Academies of Science.

2006. *Education for All Global Monitoring Report.* http://www.unesco.org/education/GMR2006/full/chapt6_eng.pdf.

2016. *Environmental Literacy.* http://www.fundee.org/.

Esbjorn-Hargens, S., Zimmerman, M.E.,. 2009. *Integral Ecology: Uniting Multiple Perspectives on the Natural World.* Boston: Integral Books.

Espinoza, Angela. Walker, Jon. 2011. *A Complexity Approach to Sustainability: Theory and Application.* London: Imperial College Press.

Francois, Charles. 1997. *International Encyclopedia of Systems and Cybernetics.* München: KG Saur.

2008. *Geosciences Literacy.* 12 17. http://www.coexploration.org/geoscienceliteracy/.

Glenn, J., FLorescu,E. 2015. *2015-16 State of the Future.* Washington D.C.: The Millenium Project.

2015. *Horizon 2020 Ocean Literacy.* https://ec.europa.eu/programmes/horizon2020/en/news/lesson-ocean-literacy.

2016. *IFSR CONVERSATION 2016 (April 2 – 8, Linz, Austria).* April 3. http://www.ifsr.org/index.php/event/ifsr-conversation-2016-april-2-8-linz-austria/.

2015. *International Society for Systems Sciences Annual Conference Berlin.* http://isss.org/world/Berlin_2015.

Ison, Ray. 2010. *Systems Practice: How to Act in Climate-Change World.* Milton Keynes: The Open University.

2012. *Literacy Decade.* http://www.unesco.org/new/en/education/themes/education-building-blocks/literacy/un-literacy-decade/.

Martin, J., Ferris, T.,. 2008. "On the Various Conceptualizations of Systems and Their Impact on the Practice of Systems Engineering." *INCOSE International Symposium* 577-593.

Mobus, G.E., Kalton, M.C. 2015. *Principles of Systems Sciences.* New York: Springer.

Nuffield Foundation. 1973. *Physical Science Introduction and Guide.* London: Penguin.

2016. *Ocean Literacy.* December 19. http://www.oceanliteracy.net.

Peters, John Beishon and Geoff. 1977. *Systems Behaviour.* London: Harper and Row.

Rousseau, D., Bellingham, J., Wilby, J., & Blachfellner, S.,. 2016. "In Search of General Systems Theory." *Systema* 76-99.

Stone, M.K., Barlow, Z. 2005. *Ecological Literacy: Educating Our Children for a Sustainable World.* San Francisco: Sierra Club Books.

2016. *Systems Science Working Group.* 12. https://sites.google.com/site/syssciwg/.

2016. *SysWeb - The Open University of Systems Group Website.* 12. http://www.sysweb.open.ac.uk.

Troncale, Len. 2013. "Systems Processes and Pathologies: Creating An Integrated Framework for Systems Science." *INOCSE International Symposium* 1330-1353.

Tuddenham, Peter. 2016. *College of Exploration Systems Literacy.* http://www.coexploration.org/systemsliteracy/incose/incose-is-2016-systems-literacy.pdf.

Tuddenham, Peter. Singer, Janet. 2016. http://www.coexploration.org/systemsliteracy/incose/3a_Systems-Literacy.pdf.

2016. *What is the IFSR?* 12 5. http://www.ifsr.org/index.php/what-is-the-ifsr/what-is-the-ifsr-2/.

2016. *World Population.* 12 31. http://www.worldometers.info/world-population/.

Wysession, M. E., D. A. Budd, K. Campbell, M. Conklin, E. Kappel, J. Karsten, N. LaDue, G. Lewis, L. Patino, R. Raynolds, R. W. Ridky, R. M. Ross, J. Taber, B. Tewksbury, and P. Tuddenham. 2012. "Developing and Applying a Set of Earth Science Literacy Principles." *Journal of Geoscience Education* 60(2), 95-99.

Team 1: Exploring Transdisciplinarity using Hierarchy Theory, Boulding's Skeleton of Science, and General Systems Theory

Jennifer Wilby, United Kingdom, j.wilby@hull.ac.uk
Stefan Blachfellner, Austria, stefan.blachfellner@bcsss.org
Sue Gabriele, USA, sgabriele@gemslearning.net
Allenna Leonard, Canada, allenna_leonard@yahoo.com
Janet Singer, USA, jwillissinger@measures.org
Michael Singer, USA mjsinger@soe.ucsc.edu

I speak a mystery: that there is no end
To greatness or to smallness. Did we shrink
To atom's size we would not reach the brink
Of manifoldness, but would see extend
A great new universe, whose atoms rend
Themselves in turn to universes: think
Ourselves but great enough, and all stars link
In one small molecule, whose tremors send
Some speck of vaster light to worlds outside
Our mote of galaxies. This greater world
Is but an atom in a greater, furled
Each one in each, endlessly multiplied.

[Boulding, in Kerman, 1974, p.9]

Boulding wrote a first draft of the above poem at sixteen and this version at thirty-one years of age. It would seem that although his training began in economics, from the days of his youth the pull towards the work of the generalist influenced his writings from the earliest of days. The purpose of our Conversation at Linz was to discuss the hierarchy of systems complexity that Kenneth E. Boulding proposed in "General Systems Theory: The Skeleton of Science" (1956), drawing on his earlier work *The Image* (1956). We sought to explore the possibilities for informing a process of intentionally holistic transdisciplinarity).

Motivation: Integration across Disciplines to Transdisciplinarity

Members of this team have been involved with research that would feed into the conversation topic during the week-long meeting in Linz (Singer, 2012; Rousseau et al, 2014, 2016 a,b,c). One output from earlier research was "The Manifesto of General Systems Transdisciplinarity (GSTD)", which begins:

"Our world and our society are in trouble. Nature's systems are complex and interconnected, yet our knowledge resides in disciplinary silos. As a result, our human activities tend to originate from within these siloed domains, and as they become increasingly impactful, the risk of unforeseen consequences becomes ever stronger. The interdependent systems we rely on for our survival and our welfare are in danger, sometimes even due to the actions we take to try to protect ourselves and our planet (2015, Rousseau et al.)."

The search for general ontology from which a transdisciplinary systemic behavior emerges is the core of an ongoing research programme in general systemology and general systems transdisciplinarity in practice. The diagram shown below in Figure 1 has been developed from the work of von Bertalanffy's (1968) GST and the overarching unity, and Laszlo's (1972) systems philosophy as the underpinning unity to show the relationships between GST, systemics, disciplines, pluralistic ontologies and a general ontology (Rousseau et al, 2014, 2016 a,b,c).

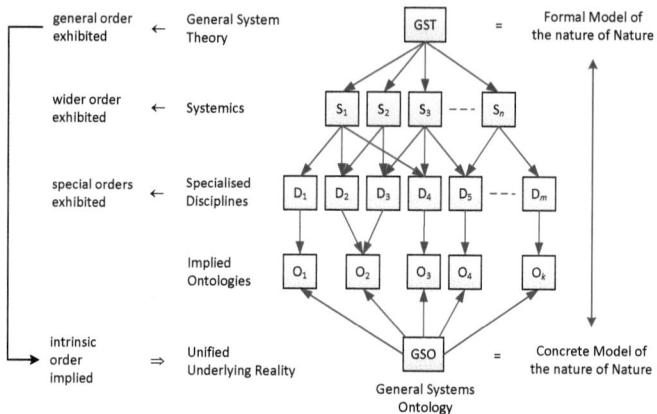

Figure 1: GST and the Unity of Knowledge (Rousseau & Wilby, 2014, p.6).

Transdisciplinarity in practice requires more than simply bringing different disciplines into an intervention (Wilby, 2010, 2011; Madni, 2007, 2010. Rousseau and Wilby (2014) argued that it will arise in practice from what could be called a General Systems Epistemology (GSE), and that development will be based on a radical change and design of practice coming from a unified single ontology (Figure 1). A unified single ontology underpinning the epistemology and development of methods could lead to a completely different form of working in disciplinarity. Individuals and methods would not simply be employed in a pluralistic melding of "better teamwork", dealing with the tensions arising when different disciplines are "put together" in practice. An initial ordering of increasing complexity in various forms of working in disciplinary practices, from mono-disciplinary practice towards the goal of transdisciplinary practice is shown in Figure 2.

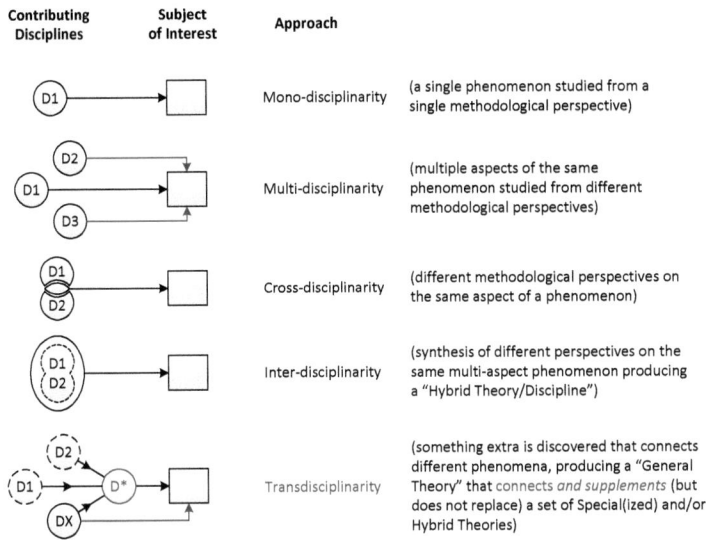

Figure 2: Kinds of Disciplinarity (adapted from (Rousseau & Wilby, 2014)

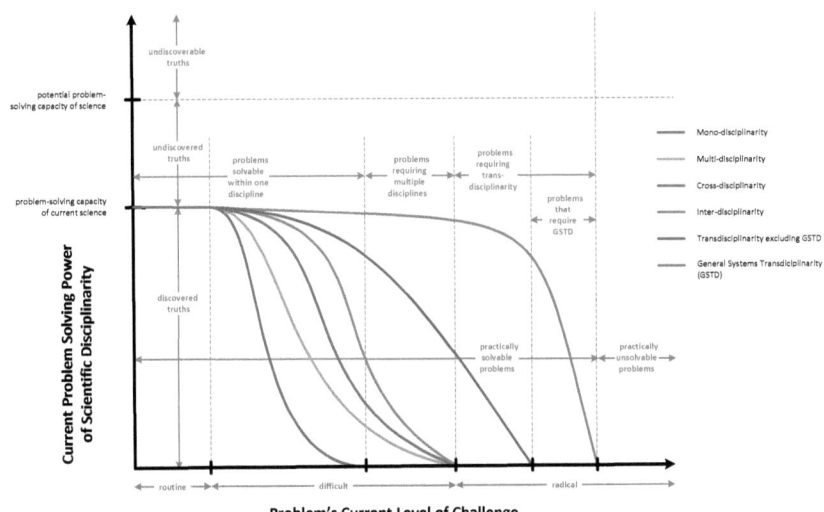

Figure 3: The application areas of kinds of disciplinarity (Rousseau, et al, 2016c)

In a recent paper, (Rousseau, et al., 2016c), the designs of disciplinarity displayed in Figure 3 have been transferred into a more dynamic relationship to show more clearly the increasing power of multiple disciplines used together in practice, while also displaying how even these combinations still approach pragmatic boundaries on each axis as to the limits of what is knowable, and what is solvable.

Figure 3 shows along the x-axis, the increasing level of challenge and increasing complexity in a problem situation, broken into 3 broad categories of routine, difficult, and radical. Known models and theories can be brought to bear on "routine" problems, but as the complexity increases, in a similar pattern displayed in Boulding's *Skeleton of Science*, then the theories and methods required to address "Difficult" and "Radical" problem situations are less certain in their application and outcomes.

"These are provisional categories, because it is never certain that a given phenomenon has been correctly or fully explained, is really readily analyzable, or actually does lie outside the analytic capacity of the given disciplinary framework. In every discipline the central objective is to maximize the scope of what can be explained, predicted, managed or utilized. Doing this calls for different kinds of disciplinarity depending on the complexity of the issue. When dealing with a specific challenge the kinds of disciplinarity are typically engaged in the order of their relative complexity, in order to find the solution in the simplest possible way. However, given the nature and range of phenomena that still lie beyond scientific explanation, it is likely that scientific investigation will increasingly call for transdisciplinary working" (Rousseau, et al, 2016c, p. 54).

In the current 2016 IFSR Conversation, the intent was to map specifically chosen systems methodologies in terms of Boulding's work, to demonstrate the systems principles incorporated (or not) in those methodologies, and where found, how those principles might be used to illuminate a possible form of a new transdisciplinarity in practice. This follows on from work undertaken at the 2012 Conversation with regard to diagrams by Singer et al. (*Systems Practice Framework*, 2012) and Wilby et al. (*Studying Systems Behaviour*, 2011). One aim in this Conversation was to examine relationships and similarities between these models, Boulding's work and newer developments in transdisciplinarity theory and practice (Rousseau, et al. 2016a,b,c). The next section presents some background on Boulding's work, and how that may be used in transdisciplinary practice.

Boulding's Skeleton (or Typology) of Science

An underlying theme in Kenneth Boulding's research and writing was the search for governing principles, rules and system structures. Boulding worked to discover some system of measurement (a form of gravimeter) applicable to the general field of social systems, similar to those found in the physical sciences. His starting point for exploring a social-systems gravimeter was the article "General Systems Theory: Skeleton of Science", written in 1956. This was a framework that Scott referred to as a typology of system complexity (Scott, 1992).

The Skeleton consists of nine levels of organization, presenting an ever-increasing complexity of organization and scale (from static structures and frameworks, to clockworks, control mechanisms (thermostats), open systems (cells), genetic-society systems (organisms), animals, humans, socio-cultural systems (organizations) and, transcendental systems (inescapable unknowables). These are shown in Figure 4, adapted from Mingers, 1997.

Level	Description	Characteristic	Type of relations	Example
1	Structures and frameworks	Static, spatial patterns	*Topology* (where)	Bridge, mountain, table, crystal
2	Single mechanistic systems	Dynamic, pre-determined changes, processes	*Order* (when)	Solar system, clock, tune, computer
3	Control mechanisms, cybernetic systems	Error-controlled feedback, information	*Specification* (what)	Thermostat, body temperature system, auto-catalytic system
4	Living systems	Continuous self-production	*Autopoietic* relations	Cell, amoeba, single-celled bacteria
5	Multicellular system	Functional differentiation	*Structural coupling* between cells (Second-order autopoiesis)	Plants, fungi, moulds, algi
6	Organisms with nervous systems	Interaction with relations	*Symbolic, abstract* relations	Most animals (except, e.g., sponges)
7	Observing systems	Language, self-consciousness	*Recursive, self-referential* relations	Humans
8	Social systems	Rules, meanings, norms, power	*Structural coupling* between organisms (third-order autopoiesis)	Families, organizations
9	Transcendental systems			

Figure 4. Mingers' Adaptation of Boulding's *Skeleton of Science* (from Mingers, 1997, p.307)

The first perception of Boulding's typology is of increasing complexity from the first to the ninth level. There are additional ways of viewing this increasing complexity:

- the increasing complexity of phenomenon themselves, which relates strongly to the development of self-awareness (Boulding's *The Image*) at each increasing level of the Skeleton,

- the increasing complexity of the systems themselves at each level; their boundaries and environments,

- the increasing complexity of modeling required for each of these systems,

- the increasing complexity of the image of the world held by each level and how that image is observer-dependent (or level-dependent) in its interpretation of its incoming messages.

It is these viewpoints on the content and context of Boulding's Skeleton this proposed conversation seeks to explore in discussion, in concert with hierarchy theory and general systems theory, to explore the realization of transdisciplinary forms of systems science, to search for the evidence of systemicity and some measurement of that concept in existing and future designs for systems methodologies.

Using Hierarchy Theory to move toward Transdisciplinarity

Within hierarchical systems, the role of the observer is a core responsibility in defining the system of interest, and thus its scale and resolution, and chosen boundaries. This determination of what constitutes the system of study, allows the application of interpretations of that system, the communication, controls, constraints and containments within and between levels. Using hierarchical concepts in concert with the images of representing and grouping complex systems as developed in Boulding's Skeleton, adds depth to hierarchical systems research.

As systems become more complex, the fuzzier the image and the more personal and individual the value filters become for those systems, and the more important the individual observer and observer self-awareness, critique and reflection becomes at those points. While Boulding's Skeleton does feel intuitively correct, the problem of increasing complexity in image, message filtering and observer-dependency at the higher levels of the Skeleton will continue to frustrate the search for a working, valuable, 'social-science gravimeter'. It is this search to which this Conversation endeavors to contribute in the development of such knowledge.

An Elaboration of Boulding's Typology: The rICE Seed for Social Systems Renewal

Team member Sue Gabriele discussed her frameworks for building relative Inclusive, Continuing, and Emancipatory (rICE) social systems starting from Boulding (1956), Scott (1992), Checkland (1991), Gabriele (1997). Examples drew from her experience and research in schools and workplaces. Her development was shared in presentations with team members and are recaptured here in Figures 5 through 9. Figure 5 shows Gabriele's elaboration of Boulding's typology, to be used as a lens for viewing social systems. Along the bottom of the figure are Boulding's nine types of system in the world. From left to right, from simple, moving to complex; each system level is composed of all the levels below it and is named by the new property that it adds. The more complex the system level, the more variability, the less predictability.

Frameworks, clockworks, and control systems or "thermostats" (levels 1-3 in Figure 5), are predictable, designable to exteriorly prescribed criteria (e.g., goals determined by a teacher, engineer, or CEO). Open, blueprint, image-aware, and symbol-processing parts (levels 4-7) are not designable. These undesignable systems, organisms, act according to interiorly prescribed criteria—needs (Level 4: e.g., amoeba or living cell), abilities (Level 5:e.g., plant), perceptions (Level 6: e.g., animal), and choices (Level 7: human) -- of increasing variability. Level 4-7 system boundaries are mandatory (illustrated with solid lines). Level 8-9 system boundaries are fleeting, optional (illustrated with dashed lines). Social and transcendent levels (Levels 8-9) are thus even more variable. Level 7 systems (humans) can ignore the leader's input and even take opposite action. Thus, Level 7 (individual) goals preempt Level 8 (organization) goals. Individual humans can move from one Level 8 system to another – changing their schools or workplaces. They cannot change their Level 7 system – their physical body.

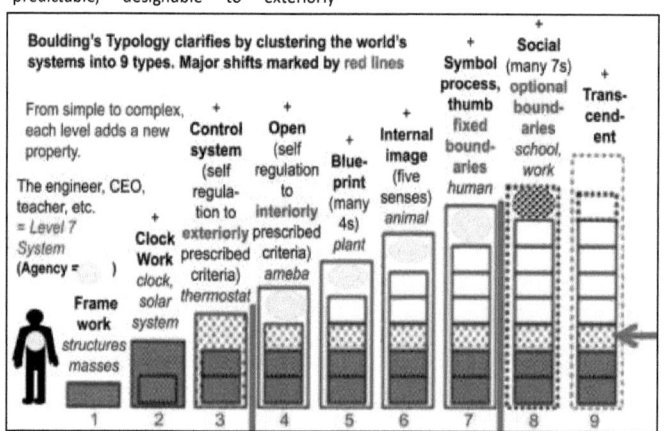

Figure 5. Boulding's Typology Elaborated

With regard to traditional management theory, Boulding's nine-level typology clarifies and unifies the two conflicting camps. In other words, top-down old paradigm bureaucratic models assume all parts of a social system are designable. New paradigm laissez-faire models assume no parts are designable. Boulding's typology shows how both paradigms are needed. Further Boulding's typology reveals which parts of a social system are designable (Levels 1-3 or Things) and which are not (Levels 4-9: People and Outcomes).

Interior agency is represented in yellow in Figure 5. Agency of behavior and learning is determined within each living organism (levels 4-7). In social systems (level 8), agency is within each individual system member resulting in infinite variability in learning and behavior. Finally, the leader, engineer, CEO or teacher (left in Figure 5) also learns and behaves according to interiorly prescribed criteria or one's image (Boulding, 1956)

.

Core Principles from this Framework

Three core principles are identified in the elaboration of Boulding's 9-Level Social System. They advance our understanding of the nature of human learning and behavior in social systems. Linking these principles to transdisciplinarity and to hierarchy theory leads us to apply them at all or multiple levels of system (vertically, cf. hierarchy theory), and across all or multiple disciplines (horizontally, cf. transdisciplinarity) and thus to break out of the silo effect.

1. A shift in agency between Levels 3 and 4 (red vertical line);

2. A shift in span of control between level 7 and 8 (red vertical line); and

3. A single most important factor in the health of an organism or social system--its adjustment capacities located at Level 3, control systems, "thermostat" system (red horizontal arrow).

The first step (1) in the path to a more fully specified new paradigm for social system behavior is this shift in agency--from teacher to learner, from CEO to employee. This shift is as dramatic and far-reaching as the earth/sun rotation paradigm shift in astronomy. Whether behavioral laws and causes relate to gravity or human agency, both paradigm shifts here are proposed as hard science--a result of extensive empirical observation, rather than speculation. A shift at such a grand level requires reconceptualization and recalculation at all levels of system. Thus, development and applications are to be wide (across disciplines: cf. transdisciplinarity) and deep (at all levels of organization: cf. hierarchy theory).

However, this agency shift in instruction/management theory is only a partial answer, leaving two conflicting camps: those who propose that the leader is sole agent and must control the supervised vs. those who argue that the supervised are agents of their own learning/performance and need total flexibility. Again, Boulding's typology shows that both control and flexibility are needed, as well as which parts require control (Levels 1-3) and which parts flexibility (Levels 4-9).

Further developing the shift that is revealed between Level 3 and 4 (Figure 5), a second and third step are gleaned out of Boulding's social system to more fully specify the nature of human learning and behavior in a social system. (2) Every human is a learner. This is true of all people in the system, both the supervised and their leaders or supervisors; and (3) there is infinite variability in individual learning and behavior. People perceive and behave each according to his or her own image. This shift, agency in the learner or worker and its infinite variability, seems unsurmountable at first. And it is unsurmountable with old paradigm "Install" thinking. It requires a shift in understanding of the leader/learner roles and relationship. We propose to unify and subsume the install and laissez-faire paradigms with the provide/pickup paradigm.

The first core principle is observed in the shift from Level 3 to level 4. Humans learn and behave according to interiorly prescribed criteria—each according to their individually variable needs (Level 4+), abilities (Level 5 +), perceptions (Level 6+), and choices (Level 7 +). This principle is true horizontally, for example in schools, workplaces, and other communities. It is true vertically, from top management to production workers, from school superintendents to educators to students).

The infinite variability in human learning and behavior can be clustered into three learning domains named cognitive, affective and psychomotor (CAP). In other words, if the leader's input is an adequate match with the learner's CAP domains, pickup will occur. If not, pickup will not occur. CAP is elaborated in later sections and illustrated in Figure 7.

The CAP pickup principle leads to in a new three-condition systems method, innovation or intervention: ICE. ICE is so named because an effective program should be inclusive, continuing and emancipatory, to provide optimal and multiple opportunities for pickup. A specific ICE program becomes rICE when generalized. The 'r' refers to relevance and relativity, which might differ slightly across disciplines and at different levels of organization. A rICE Methodology has the elements to become a new form of transdisciplinarity in practice (horizontal view) as well as an application that can be used at all levels of organization (a hierarchical or vertical view). The rICE methodology is elaborated in Figure 9.

Second and third core principles were not developed. The second principle occurs in the shift from Boulding's Level 7 to 8. Level 7 needs are mandatory and Level 8 needs are optional. One suggested shift is a reconceptualization in management theory from span of control to span of pickup. The third principle is observed in the Level 3 control system across all complex systems, Level 3 and above. It reveals the one single key to a system's effectiveness is its adjustment capacities.

Continuing the development and implications of the first core principle, Figure 6 lays out the path to the provide/pickup paradigm, along with some transdisciplinary and hierarchical aspects. Bottom left in Figure 6, old directive assumptions are that leaders (P) are sole agents and install knowledge (K) into those they lead (pp). The limits of old directive assumptions have led to laissez-faire assumptions: learners and workers (pp) as sole agents (bottom center in Figure 6). However, this has left the leader's role unclear. For example, does the leader distinguish between excellent and mediocre work, or praise both equally?

Top left, a unifying paradigm inspired by Boulding's typology reveals that all people—leaders (P) and those they lead (pp)--are agents of their own learning and behavior

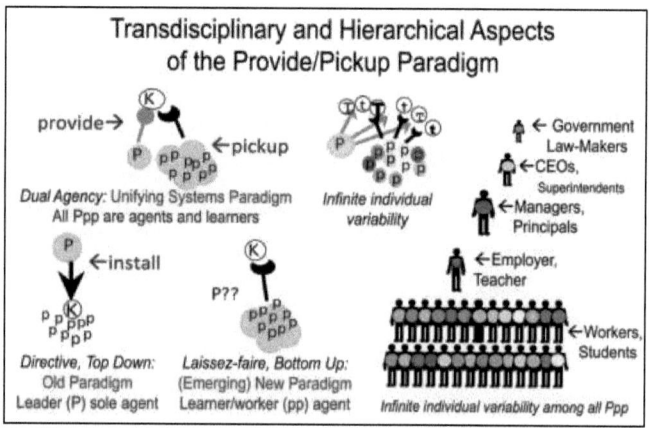

Figure 6. The Provide/Pickup Paradigm

Top center in Figure 6 illustrates the infinite variability in everyone's image, learning and behavior (agency in multiple colors). It follows that the leader or teacher is to provide information, activities, tasks (T) in a variety of ways. Students and workers pick up information

(T) and develop skills and mastery each at their own rate. Principles of the provide/pickup paradigm apply wide—to people across all disciplines. Right is a final illustration of this variability in large social systems. Leaders, learners, workers, each and all have a different interior criteria or image (agency in different colors) which guides their learning and behavior. These principles apply deep—at all levels of organization.

Downshifting the unit of focus from the organization, and the pair, to the individual, this infinite variability is helpfully clustered into three domains. Bott's work in adult learning theory (1995) explains that learning will occur, and tasks will be achieved, if the assignment or task is an adequate match with the learner's/worker's cognitive, affective, and psychomotor domains (CAP domains). Likewise, Patterson and Covey (2002) propose that workers will do what is asked of them on the condition that they are willing and able. Combining this insight with the three learning domains, we see that learners/workers must be 1) able mentally (cognitive); 2) able physically (psychomotor); and 3) willing (affective).

In a nutshell, teachers then are not to teach, leaders are not to lead. They are to provide CAP appropriate opportunities for learner/worker pickup. Leaders do have to multitask: They have to adjust (like a thermostat - Boulding's level 3 system) between doing their own work, and monitoring the room/building to notice when someone is off-task, where pickup has not occurred. They then help the system member identify the block preventing pickup. A block might be cognitive: For example, the learner or worker doesn't understand the task. It might be affective: For example, he/she does not see the importance of the new task and has set it aside to continue other work. A block might be physical/psychomotor: For example, he/she needs glasses and cannot read the small font of the document. It might be a mixture: For example, the worker didn't eat breakfast, cannot concentrate, and also thinks the project is unimportant, not useful, or even flawed (Gabriele 2014). Of course, learner and workers also multitask and adjust. They do their work, and when there is a block, they might stop and reread the instructions, or look up definitions in a dictionary.

Pickup is only the first step in learner or worker response. The old paradigm is that the leader directs or installs information in the learner or employee. The more fully specified new paradigm is that the leader provides information for the learners to pick up, who do so each at their own pace, according to their own perceptions and purposes. After pickup comes, learning, mastery, and/or performance. The focus here is pickup, however, because pickup is the concept that needs highlighting. Pickup is where the key breakdown occurs.

Pickup, Throughput, Output, and Links to Boulding

Figure 7 illustrates the structures and processes of pickup and output and those in between (throughput). The unit of focus is the individual. Figure 7(left) illustrates three main pickup points (in red): the eyes, ears and hands.

Figure 7 (middle) downshifts from outside of the individual to inside the individual. Pickup occurs when there is an adequate match of the input to the individual's CAP domains: cognitive (dark gray); affective (yellow); and psychomotor (light gray). Depending on each individual, it may be followed by learning, mastery, creativity, and action/performance. If there is not an adequate match or serious mismatch, the individual may not notice, ignore, misinterpret, or display fight, flight or submit responses.

Figure 7 (right) upshifts from inside the individual to outside the individual again. Pickup is followed by individually variable throughput, and then results in even more variable outputs. Figure 7C illustrates three main output points (in red): the mouth, hands, and feet.

Links to Boulding in Figure 7 are as follows: Level 1 frameworks in the pickup through output processes are eyes, ears, hands, mouth, feet; and also, inside the individual, the cognitive, affective and psychomotor domains. Pickup, when automatic, is mainly a Level 2 clockwork process as are circulation, respiration, and digestion. Level 3 is a control system, an ON/OFF switch. When there is a CAP match, the process is ON and pickup occurs. When there is a CAP block, the process turns OFF and pickup doesn't occur or is skewed. Levels 4 – 7 add non-clockwork processes determined by interiorly prescribed criteria. In other words, at Level 7, pickup is determined by each individual's image, his or her willingness (affective), and ability (cognitive and psychomotor). Throughputs and outputs are non-clockwork.

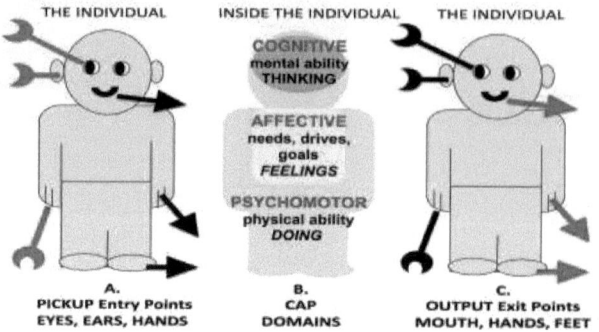

Figure 7. From Pickup to Output at the Level of the Individual

Links to Hierarchy Theory and Transdisciplinarity

These new or clarified factors are [1] agency within each system member, [2] infinite variability in each system member's image, learning and behavior, and [3] a resulting new Provide/Pickup paradigm for the leader/learner relationship. These shifts, complexities and variabilities require adaptable and meaningful applications wide (across disciplines: cf. transdisciplinarity) and deep (at all levels of organization: cf. hierarchy theory). If this is not achieved, our knowledge will remain in silos.

Figure 8 illustrates more specific areas for linking insights of agency and pickup from Boulding's Typology to Hierarchy Theory and Transdisciplinarity. Left are examples of eight disciplines. There are the hard technical systems, where material agency dominates (Levels 1-3 in Boulding's Typology), and there are the soft social systems, where human agency dominates. Informed by transdisciplinarity, knowledge and concepts are to be meaningful, to make sense, across all the disciplines. Figure 8 shows examples of physical systems of institutions and organizations. Informed by hierarchy theory, knowledge and concepts are to be meaningful, to make sense, at all levels of organization.

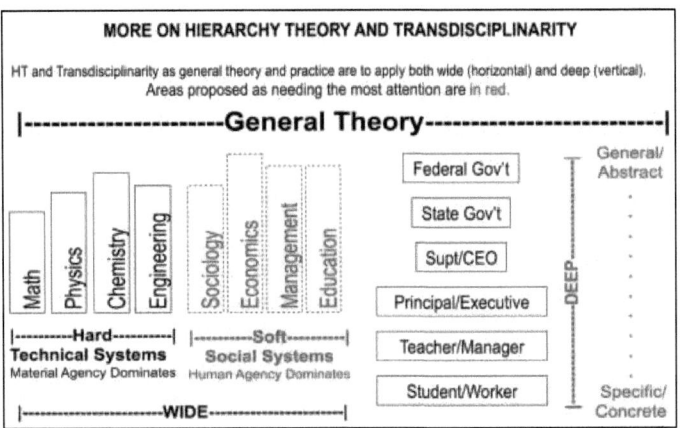

Figure 8. Illustrations of Hierarchy Theory and Transdisciplinarity

Far right is another dimension and continuum, from general and abstract to specific and concrete. Boulding affirmed that "Somewhere however between the specific that has no meaning and the general that has no content there must be, for each purpose and at each level of abstraction, an optimum degree of generality" (1956, 197). Thus, specific concepts and vocabulary are to be appropriately general or specific to be most meaningful at each level of organization and within each discipline.

Certain well-known words and concepts, however, transcend boundaries. Such terms are useful bridges. An example is expert or expertise. The terms expert and expertise are known across all disciplines, and at all levels of organization. Reframing expertise to include assumptions of agency shift and pickup would serve to help transcend silo knowledge and advance the new principles associated with agency shift and the provide/pickup paradigm. Gabriele writes:

"Experts are those who are authorized or credentialed in a specific field. They are also intimately involved with their subject matter, due to spending a long time with it, seeing it under many conditions. …. In the field of education, teachers are the key experts in classroom procedures, principals in school procedures, parents in their specific children's needs and goals, educational researchers in educational theory, and educational lawyers and policy makers in educational law and mandates. Efforts to improve, design, or redesign schools must meet the standards of all these experts" (2014, p. 56).

Towards A New Approach to Social System Change: A Seed for Systemic Renewal

An initial formula or representation of a new social system methodology informed by principles of the provide/pickup paradigm is illustrated in Figure 9. To maximize the power of a high quality innovation or intervention (T) to effect systemic change in an implementation or study, it needs three desirable, optimal (or necessary and sufficient) conditions: it is designed to be inclusive, continuing, and emancipatory (ICE). In this way, it increases members' opportunities for pickup, learning, and mastery. Goals of systemic change are reframed as goals of systemic renewal, and the rICE framework is usefully viewed both as a seed to be planted inside the system and a process nurtured.

The three dimensions and axes of Figure 9 are labeled: from the left, Inclusive (axis Z), Continuing (axis X), and Emancipatory (axis Y). Note that the three conditions ICE in a specific example become rICE in the general premise (toward a general theory), adding an r (relativity) factor. Relativity is defined as depending on other factors that vary according to context. The four elements of ICE and examples of the r factor are elaborated next.

I= Inclusive: Designed to serve (1) the whole person (the face at the origin of the axes in Figure 9); (2) the whole group—each person in the room, class, or meeting; (3) the whole building or school; (4) the whole school district or organization, in (5) the whole city, state, or country, and (6) the whole world. Axis Z is a first dimension and a space view (also Boulding's system level 1, a designable Thing). The measure of Inclusivity might be attained by these study questions: First, in what ways and to what degree is design of the input inclusive? Designed for everyone in the system? Second, to what degree and in what ways do the outcomes match, surpass, fall short of, or differ from the inclusivity traits in the design? Third, to what degree has everyone in each group, and all groups in the system, been included at the end of the study?

C = Continuing: Regularly revisited (e.g., in auditory review routines), daily, weekly, or monthly (small black arrows pointing up to the X-axis in Figure 9); and always accessible (e.g., wall charts or at the fingertips of users, (e.g. in user manuals, -- e-learning or traditional). Axis X is a second dimension and a time view (also Boulding's system level 2, a designable Thing). Measures of Continuity might be achieved with these questions: First, Does the design of the input build in the continuity traits? Is the input designed to be reviewed weekly? monthly? Second, Is the outcome continuous? To what degree and in what ways do the outcomes match, surpass, fall short of, or differ from the continuity dimension in the design? Third, at the end of the study, did the users actually have review routines weekly, monthly?

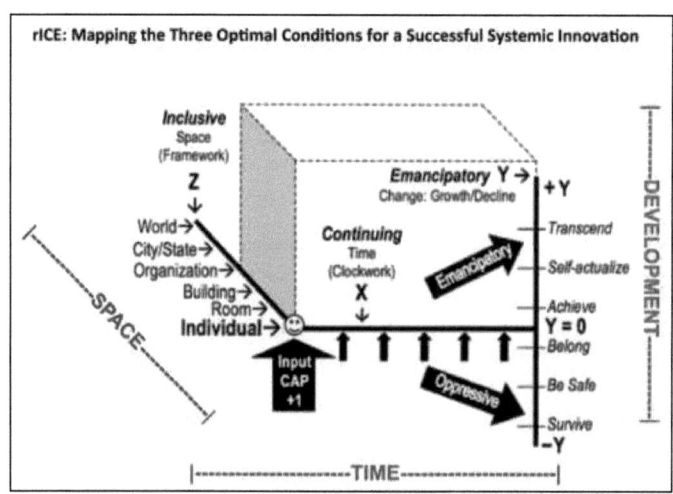

Figure 9. The ICE or rICE Design and Evaluation Methodology

E = Emancipatory: Unshackling and accelerating positive development. Axis Y is a third dimension and an outcome view (also Boulding's system levels 7–9 functioning). Figure 9 illustrates this condition, and its opposite, in two arrows labeled emancipatory and oppressive.

On the right of the figure is Maslow's hierarchy as a loose guide (Maslow in Valle, 1989). In other words, if system members are able to use their energy to achieve, self-actualize, and/or transcend, this suggests the emancipatory condition. If system members have to use their energy to belong, feel safe, or survive, this suggests the oppressive condition. The condition of emancipatory is not designable; it is emergent. However, aspects of the emancipatory condition are designable because program quality or input (thick black arrow pointing up in Figure 9) is designable.

Program Quality and System Level/Type. There are two designable conditions (T) that are assumed before application of the ICE or rICE premise. First, the input (intervention or program) is high quality, which includes what will now be abbreviated as CAP and CAP +1. That is, the cognitive, affective, and psychomotor (CAP) match of the input is appropriate for system members, plus a right amount of advance and challenge with new information or skills (+1). Examples are as follows.

Cognitive: Students have learned the geography of their country and hemisphere. Now they are learning world geography. The science department teachers have achieved the fine-tuning of their tenth-grade course of study. They are now working on eleventh-grade.

Affective: It is the beginning of the year, and for three weeks now, I (as teacher) have been consciously and carefully building trust with my new students (e.g., trust that my lessons are valuable, trust that I will treat my students fairly and with respect). I can now be a little more relaxed, perhaps a little less formal or more affectionate, as I have achieved a healthy learning environment and a good connection with the students.

Psychomotor: Primary school children have learned to use a pencil and pen. They then learn to write the letters of the alphabet. Their psychomotor skills for printing and writing increase at each grade level.

The formula CAP +1 is overly simple and general, but a useful guide and organizing principle. The CAP +1 abbreviation builds on Krashen's input hypothesis (1989). His formula, i + 1 (comprehensible input plus one), explains that students make progress in learning a new language when the input contains language that is slightly more advanced than their current level of comprehension.

Adding the r factor to ICE, for the acronym rICE, represents the need for ICE specifics that are relative to the systems' traits and users' needs and conditions. Some examples follow.

- rI = Relative inclusion, e.g. in today's movie rating system designed to help parents decide whether a film is appropriate for their family. From most inclusive to least inclusive, the ratings are: G, for a general audience including children; PG, parental guidance suggested; PG-13, parental guidance suggested for children under 13; R, under 17 requires accompanying parent or guardian; and NC-17, no one under 17 is admitted.

- rC = Relative continuity depends on the properties and purposes of the social system, e.g. a rICE program in a classroom might be daily or weekly. In a workplace, it might be monthly.

- rE = Relative emancipatory purposes and measures, e.g., student love of learning and worker job satisfaction. These are specific higher level goals (a la Maslow in Figure 9) of the individual and the individual's social systems.

Follow On Work

Given the complexity and scope of our topics, as well as our different images and viewpoints, there are many possibilities. We are open to their emergence. We do anticipate exploration and development of two remaining core principles identified in Gabriele's elaboration of Boulding's typology, not yet developed during our work. We propose to explore them and link them to Hierarchy Theory and Transdisciplinarity and also to treat the three core principles together, in an intentionally holistic approach.

Core Principle # 1. One possibility would be to continue refining and developing the principles illuminated by the differences between Boulding's Level 3 Level 4, the differences between Control Systems, which are self-regulating to an exteriorly-prescribed criteria, and People, self-regulating to interiorly prescribed criteria. What does this look like at all levels of organization? Individual, pair, room, building, multisite institution, city, country, world? And what does this look like in education, management, economics, politics, health care, environmental engineering, and so forth?

Core Principle # 2. We could explore another great shift occurring between Boulding's Level 7 and 8 (see Figure 5). Level 7 human systems have mandatory boundaries. Level 8 social system boundaries are optional. Significantly, the pickup paradigm allows us to reframe the concept of span of control in management theory to span of pickup, especially important in large social systems.

Core Principle # 3. We could look at the control system, present is Levels 4-9 systems arrow in Figure 5), as the key to effective systems, with regard to the importance of adjustment capacities, responsivity, or agility in these systems. We expect to link them across disciplines and throughout the organization.

Another possibility is noticing and identifying concepts that already have wide, popular meaning and/or strong transfer power and then build on them. An example mentioned in this paper is the concept of expert and expertise. Another example is the bottom line, which has meaning at all levels of system and across systems. This makes it easy to introduce the concept of triple bottom line. Regarding a core concept here, the term pickup really only has wide meaning when linked to physical pickup. For example, a person picks up milk at the supermarket. The concept of cognitive pickup is not as familiar though used, e.g., by Neisser in 1976. The concept of affective pickup is even less recognizable.

Conclusions of the Conversation and Further Development of Work

Further conversation within the Team is ongoing to explore the relationships between Boulding's typology and the search for the evidence of transdisciplinary systemicity and some measurement of that concept in specific systems methodologies. Methodologies such as Soft Systems Methodology (SSM), the Viable System Model (VSM), System Dynamics (SD), and Complex Adaptive Systems (CAS) have yet to be evaluated for systemic principles incorporated (or not) in those methodologies, and where found, how those principles might be used to illuminate a new form of transdisciplinary practice, e.g. the rICE methodology.

Team 1: Janet Singer, Allenna Leonard, guest contributor Peter Tuddenham, Sue Gabriele, Michael Singer, Stefan Blachfellner. (Team Leader Jennifer Wilby not pictured)

Acknowledgements

The authors would like to thank Peter Tuddenham, Debora Hammond and David Rousseau for their thoughtful contributions to the team discussions during the week and in the writing of this report.

References

Bott, P. (1995). *Testing and Assessment in Occupational and Technical Education*. Allyn & Bacon, Boston, MA.

Boulding, K. E. (1956). General Systems Theory: The Skeleton of Science, *Management Science*, 2, 197-208.

Boulding, K. E. (1956). *The Image: Knowledge in Life and Society*, Ann Arbor Paperbacks, The University of Michigan Press.

Checkland, P. (1981). *Systems thinking, systems practice*. John Wiley and Sons, New York.

Gabriele, S. (1997). Boulding's typology elaborated: A framework for understanding school and classroom systems. *Systems Practice*, 10(3), 271–304.

Gabriele, S. (2014). *New Hope for Schools: Findings of a Teacher turned Detective*. iUniverse.

Jackson, M.C. (2003). *Systems Thinking: Creative Holism for Managers*, John Wiley & Sons, Chichester, UK.

Jackson, M. C. and Keys, P. (1984). Towards a system of systems methodologies. *Journal of Operations Research Society*, 35, 473-86.

Kerman, C. E. (1974). *Creative Tension: The Life and Thought of Kenneth Boulding*, Ann Arbor: The University of Michigan Press.

Krashen, S. (1989). We acquire vocabulary and spelling by reading: Additional evidence for the input hypothesis. *The Modern Language Journal*, 73, 440–464.

Laszlo E. (1972). *Introduction to Systems Philosophy: Toward a New Paradigm of Contemporary Thought*. Gordon & Breach, New York, NY.

Madni, A. M. (2007). Transdisciplinarity: Reaching beyond disciplines to find connections. *Journal of Integrated Design and Process Science*, 11(1), 1-11.

Madni, A. M. (2010). Transdisciplinary system science: Implications for healthcare and other problems of global significance. *Transdisciplinary J Engineering Science*, 1(1), 38-53.

Mingers, J. (1997). Systems topologies in the light of autopoiesis: A reconceptualization of Boulding's hierarchy, and a typology of self-referential systems", Systems Research and Behavioral Science, 14 (5), pp. 303-314.

Neisser, U. (1976). *Cognition and Reality: Principles and Implications of Cognitive Psychology*, W. H. Freeman, New York.

Patterson, K., & Covey, S. (2002). *Crucial Conversations: Tools for talking when stakes are high*. McGraw-Hill, New York.

Rousseau, D., & Wilby, J. M. (2014). Moving from Disciplinarity to Transdisciplinarity in the Service of Thrivable Systems. *Systems Research and Behavioral Science*, 31(5), 666–677.

Rousseau, D., Wilby, J. M., Billingham, J. & Blachfellner, S. (2016a). A Typology for the Systems Field. *Systema*, 4(1)

Rousseau, D., Wilby, J. M., Billingham, J., & Blachfellner, S. (2016b). Manifesto for General Systems Transdisciplinarity. *Systema*, 4(1).

Rousseau, D., Wilby, J. M., Billingham, J., & Blachfellner, S. (2016c). The Scope and Range of General Systems Transdisciplinarity. *Systema*, 4(1).

Scott, W. (1986). *Organizations: Rational, natural and open systems*. Prentice Hall, Englewood Cliffs, NJ.

Singer, J., Sillitto, H., Bendz, J., Chroust, G., Hybertson, D., Lawson, H.W., Martin, J., Martin, R., Singer, M., & Takaku, T. (2012). The Systems Praxis Framework, included in *Systems and Science at Crossroads – Sixteenth IFSR Conversation*, Linz, Austria.

Valle, R. & Halling, S. (1989). *Existential-phenomenological Perspectives in Psychology: Exploring the breadth of human experience*. Plenum Press, New York.

Wilby, J. (2007). *Hierarchy Theory: A narrative critique*, unpublished PhD thesis, University of Hull.

Wilby, J. (2011). Essay: A new framework for viewing the philosophy, principles and practice of systems science. *Systems Research and Behavioral Science*, 28(5), 437-442.

Wilby J., Macaulay L., & Theodoulidis, B. (2011). Intentionally holistic knowledge intensive service systems, *International Journal of Services, Technology and Management* 16(2): 126–140.

# Team 2: Unity in Diversity – Making the Implicit Explicit

Brigitte Daniel Allegro, Co-Team Leader, France - brigitte.daniel.allegro@gmail.com
Gary Smith, Co-Team Leader, United Kingdom - gary.smith@persescomms.com
Maria Stella Castro de Lobos, Brazil - clobo@hucff.ufrj.br
Gerhard Chroust, Austria - gerhard.chroust@jku.at
Florian Daniel, France - i.daniel.florian@gmail.com
Gordon Dyer, United Kingdom - gordon.dyer@btinternet.com
Xijin Tang, China - xjtang@iss.ac.cn

Overview

The main objective of Team 2 ("Unity In Diversity – make the implicit explicit") was to design a tangible prototype of a game aiming at facilitating the acquisition of systems thinker's skills in private or professional contexts.

The proposed framework to start with (and to be challenged during the conversation) was the *Systems Tree* which highlights systems thinker's attitudes and key systems concepts. The prototype would enable:

- In terms of understanding systems concepts, to avoid wordings but rather to use tangible objects which represent concepts in such a way that makes sense for anybody (e.g. from any cultural background, independent of the mother language).

- to practice systems thinker's attitudes by play-acting diverse situations to progress through experiences and reflections towards a collective understanding. These attitudes would be developed by playing a game, using the explicit / tangible systems concepts.

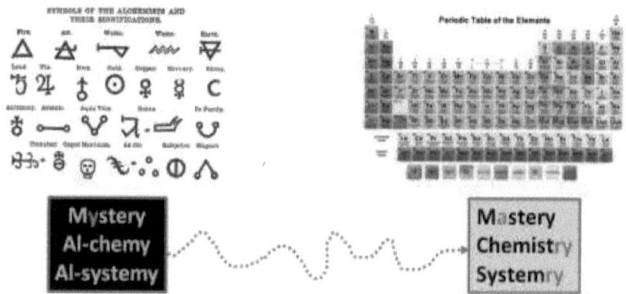

"The chemist uses their understanding of chemical elements when they interact with chemical substances. Likewise, in the future the systemist will use their understanding of systemic concepts when they manipulate and transform systems"

A key criterion of the framework being that it could be universal ("Unity" in Diversity) and engaging for everyone. By developing such a framework it was hoped that this would thus contribute to the overall theme of the 2016 Conversation 'Systems Literacy'.

The report consists of three parts:

- Part 1: The initial proposal, containing some of the concepts upon which the conversation in the Team was based

- Part 2: The executive summary: A short description of the sequence of events and processes during the week in St. Magdalena.

- Part 3: The compilation of the team members' individual reflections about the conversation. These personal reflections were written by individual team member a few weeks after the conversation itself, between April and May 2016, with some recent updates.

(See also IFSR Newsletter vol 33 (2016), no. 2, pp. 14-16)

Part 1 - The initial proposal (with some later amendments)

The world is arguably becoming more complex and the anthroposphere and biosphere increasingly interdependent and fragile. Despite the efforts of many systemic organisations it seems that our capability to synthesise and cooperate across disciplines and domains is not yet sufficient to respond effectively to global systemic stress and resultant crises.

We postulate that it is in this time of crisis that we must break down the barriers to communication across disciplines, organisations, societies, beliefs and cultures in order to promote collective understanding for a common good. In order to "de-construct" the Tower of Babel we had in mind to start a conversation about "**Unity in Diversity**".

We would like to perceive the "**Diversity**" of our world: the diversity of people with their own knowledge, ideas, beliefs, information; diversity of languages, world views; diversity of ways of thinking and working; diversity of structures, diversity of resources, diversity of systems (natural systems, socio-technico-eco systems) and to consider the "Diversity" as a huge reservoir of potentials able to build a conceptual model to facilitate a collective understanding.

We would like to define a "**Unity** in the Diversity" as not underlining the diversity but rather value it for the emergence of something that we could collectively create during the conversation. The unity could come from binding forces which could create a system.

Since art is a means to "make visible", to show, to give ways of perceiving reality or emotions (*whether in paintings, plastic arts, literature, poems, music or dance*), the artist develops skills to integrate and synthesize with the art of seeing. Since an artist is by essence systemic, we would like to use art to develop the "**In**" within the topic "Unity in Diversity".

We see this Conversation as a piece of jazz music or jazz dance where each player plays with his/her instrument, shares some basics enabling connections to be able to improvise, has different postures, and where all the players together will start, develop and conclude the piece of jazz.

The framework will be the "*Systems tree*" which is a conceptual model of the "*systems thinker's attitudes*" and the key "*systems concepts*" that facilitate system understanding.

Roles will be distributed to each member of the team utilizing different paradigms of team construction (for example colored hats, Belbin roles, archetypes, etc.). The team will be asked to consider different real world complex problems and to formalize the progression towards a collective system understanding which we refer to as "*the rules of the game*".

At the end of the week the team will construct the board, the icons for the players and define "*the rules of the game*". As an option the other teams will be invited to play the game.

Some of our initial thinking about the topic of Unity in Diversity is shown in the mind map below

In order for the conversation to have sufficient diversity to succeed in its objectives of creating a framework that might be universally applicable we produced a mind map to guide us in the selection of team members. With a diversity in professions, cultures, age and backgrounds, diverse hobbies and interests, diverse skills, yet with common behaviours and attitudes in systems 'being', team working, practical, adaptable and sharing.

The Systems tree provided a initial candidate framework for the systemic concepts. The branches representing the attitudes or mind set of the systems thinker. The roots being the "elementary" concepts of systems that systemists think about.

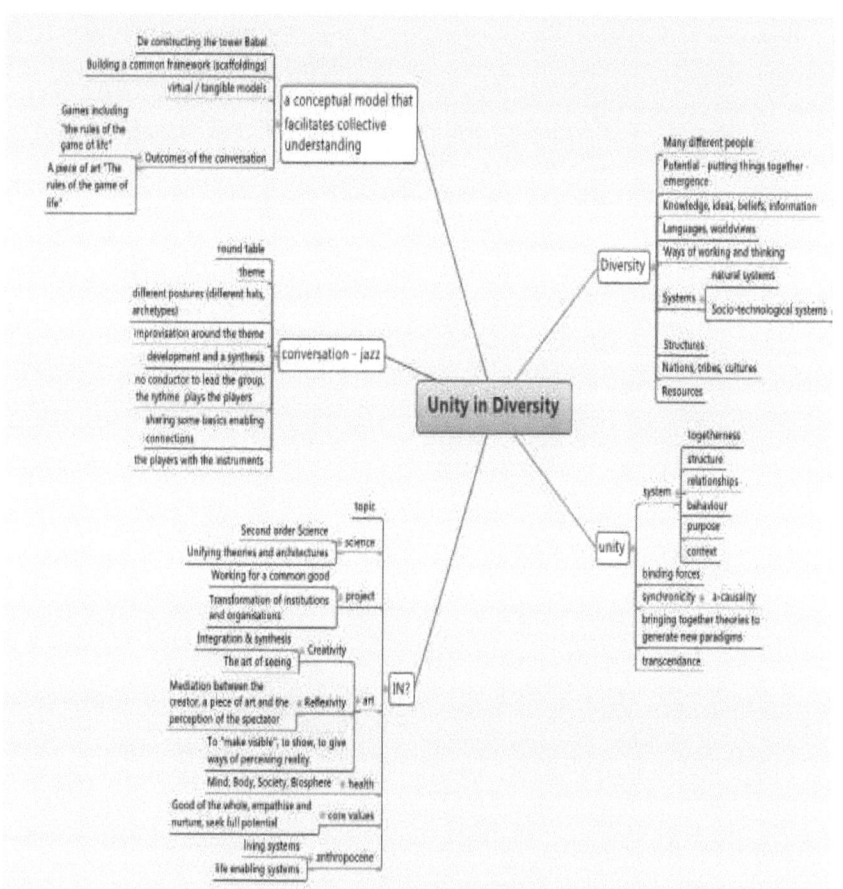

Figure 1 – Unity In Diversity Mind Map

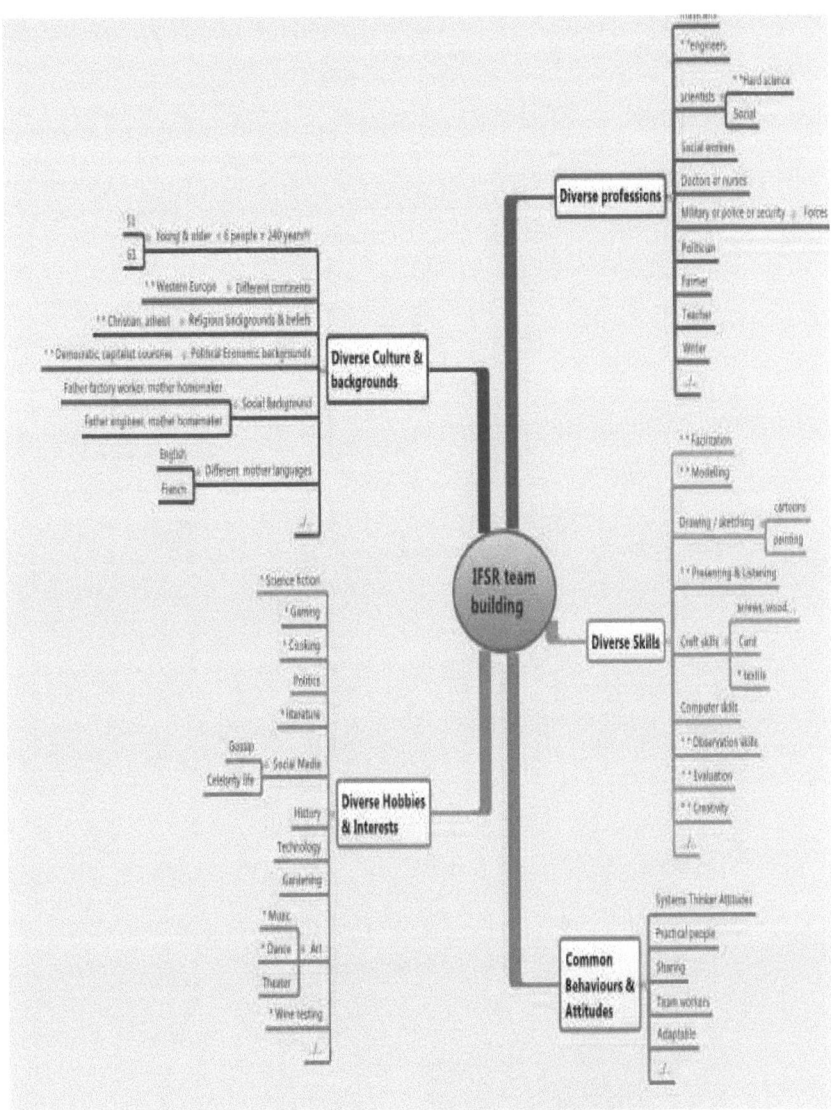

Figure 2 – Criteria of "Unity" and "Diversity" to build the team

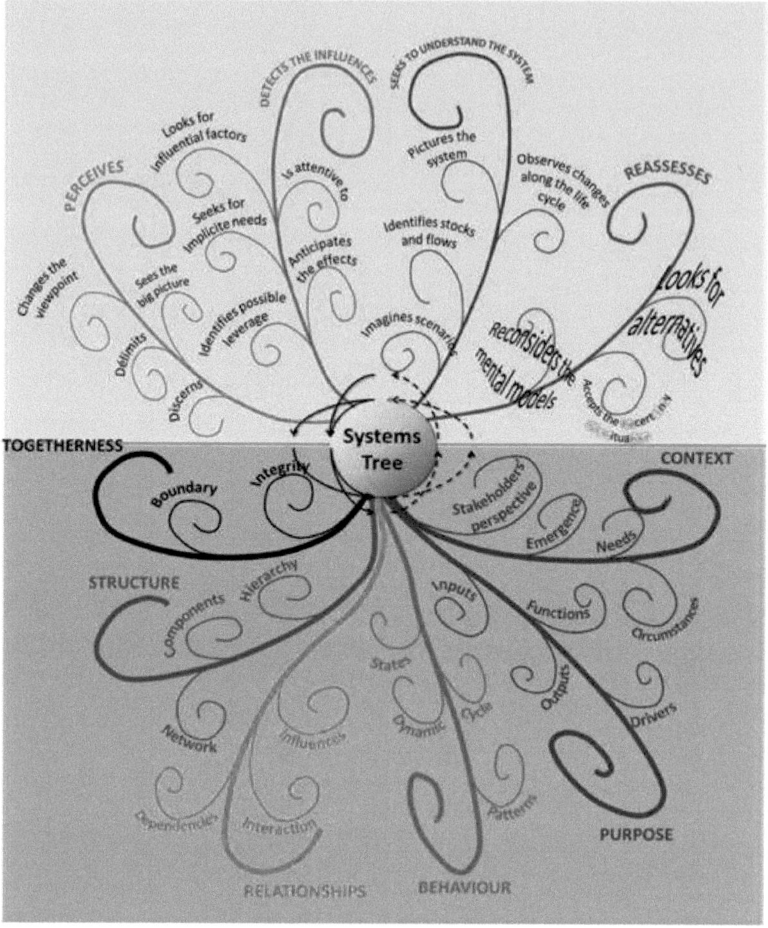

Figure 3 – The "Systems tree"

Team 2 meeting with Peter

Part 2: The Conversation process

The journey started with the team a few weeks before the actual conversation in Linz: some e-mails were exchanged, some "exercises" done by the team; contributed papers were received to generate some ideas. We had a long video call with one member of the team and a short one with most of the other members.

The Team Leaders also distributed as a basis for communication the "Systems tree" (figure 3) for analysis and for translation in natural languages. The idea was to explore these concepts, to develop a common understanding of their meaning and to have some experience in using them to consider different real world complex problems. This would allow us to develop a prototype game for teaching, exercising and developing systems thinking skills for all, which could be tuned to the diversity of the potential players.

Shortly before the start of the Conversation the team leaders laid out a framework for the days in terms of team experience that that we wanted to achieve:

- Sharing, playing and visualizing the system concepts
- Using the system concepts to analyse stories
- Building the framework for the game
- Using the game to analyse a real world problem

This was intended to facilitate the capture of the diversity of the team in the development of the toolbox for the prototype game.

Our first half day in the team did not go so well. One of the team members challenged the rigidity of the predefined schedule, and the usefulness of designing a board game as the ultimate goal of the Conversation together with and a lack of discussion of the objectives of the game After what seemed to be an impasse, Gordon suggested to use a story called "The Baron and Baroness" as a way to exercise systems thinking (see Fig. 4). Playing and discussing this game promoted a better atmosphere for conversation and to get to know each other a little better.

Fig. 4 The Baron-Baroness-game

A plot for the ‚SysteMystery' game

(to keep the surprise factor only some essential cornerstones of the plot are described)

The Plot:
- The story is set in a castle.
- It describes a series of events and interactions
- It involves 6 persons :
  - a Baron
  - a Baroness
  - 4 further persons
- Each person somehow contributes to the final killing of the Baroness.

The task:
The participants have to discuss and to judge the responsibility and blame of each individual persons for the killing the Baroness. Different answers are possible

---

After lunch, we all produced some drawings of concepts which somehow helped in sharing the idea that we can express concepts not just in words but also through art. For example when we played with the concept of boundary there were several different representations which highlighted different features of personal perspective.

On day two, we started with a systems thinking roundtable. This gave the opportunity for everyone to speak and to express what were their hopes and expectations for the conversation. The questions asked were: "What is Systems thinking? What are the challenges and what are your hopes? What situations have your left behind and what might happen here that could be valuable for you back home?"

During the second day we shared some more stories and we also took the time to explore the Chinese characters related to system concepts (see also page XXX). By the end of this day, we had agreed what the nature of the game would be in terms of qualities and framework. Its scalability and the idea that it's scaling and tailoring could be made using the concepts in relationship to the stories and games already embedded in culture.

On the third day we were joined by Peter Tuddenham and we ran a round table on the topic of "What can you do to support systems literacy?". We also then reran the "Baron-and-Baroness" plot but this time as observers.

We then started to fill in a matrix of system concepts and related simple questions that could be asked in relationship to simple stories. We also used an Aesop tale – "the cock and the jewel". We focused here on questions that could be asked to young children of age 3-5. What we realized is that dependent on the level of systems experience we could use the language and use questions scalable to the level of the player. What we also realized was that some concepts were more applicable to simple situations, whilst others were more attributable to complex situations. What we also came to appreciate was the richness of cultural stories for teaching systemic thinking and how our framework could tap into these at school or at home.

By the end of day three we had a better idea of what we might be able to achieve (see below):

Desired Scalability and Adaptability

To draw on the **stories** and **games** that are already **deeply established in the culture.**

Stories, poems and games our parents and grandparents taught us.
These often have a meaning/value that is not always immediately explicit.
When you reflect on them you develop some systemist's skills.

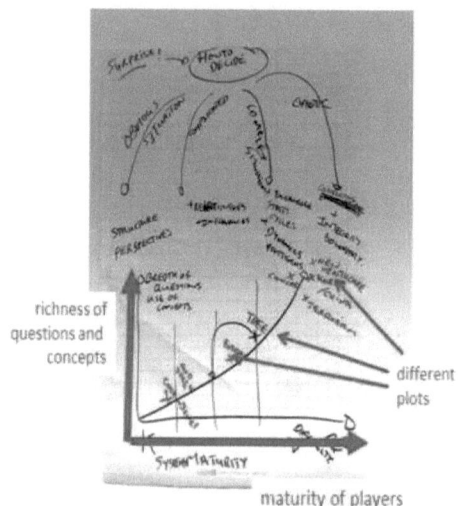

On the fourth day we started again with another round table on the topic of "Unity in Diversity". We finished a document that described the overview of the game, incorporating the "Baron-and-Baroness" plot as the example.

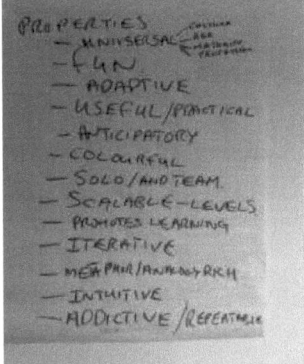
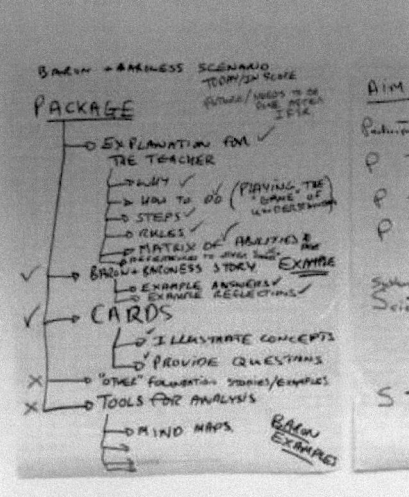

The team came up with the idea to produce a digital platform for capturing system concepts, related information such as visualization and questions. These questions where designed and related the level of the situation (simple, complicated, complex and "wicked").

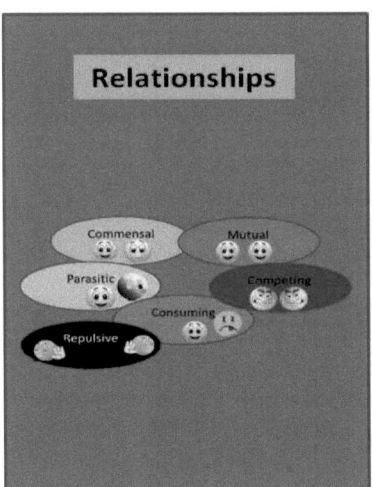

QUESTIONS
Simple
Can you describe the obvious relationships between some elements?
Complicated
How are the relationships effecting the situation?
Complex
What small changes in relationships might have big effects on the situation?
Chaotic
Is that anything about the relationships that is driving you to think that this is a chaotic situation?

The team worked very quickly in the afternoon to define digital cards and questions for many of the system concepts. Everyone was able to work within the proposed framework and made very strong contributions. In the evening we finished the presentation for the next day

As a result of the discussion we have made some adaptions to the original *Systems Tree* framework. Some concepts were renamed and some others were added. In the end we had accomplished pretty much what we aimed at, but the effort and the emotional involvement was much more difficult than expected. Also the prototype game (named "SystemMystery") was different to what the team leaders initially expected, digital instead of a tangible art. This proved to be enabler for development in an adaptable, collaborative way, thus providing a better framework for teaching, developing and practicing "Systemry" (the study of systems) that would be scalable and adaptable to a diversity of users and cultures.

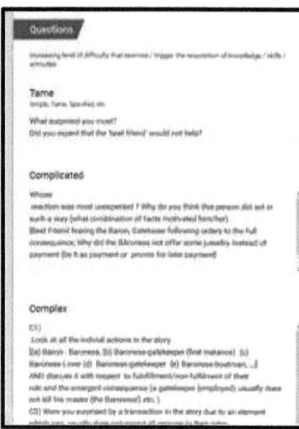

A fundamental idea was that we did not implement one specific 'gaming scenario' but rather that any story of work, play or learning experience could inserted into the platform. The "Baron-and—Baroness" plot was just one of that we played with during our prototyping. Sources for experiences can be fables, fairy tales, games, real world problems at home or at work – a viable tool for systems engineers and problem solvers.

The essential outcome of the team's effort being a prototype toolbox that could be used as a platform for understanding and applying System Thinking in a variety of contexts.

> We wanted to developing a **toolbox** in order to contribute to **Systems Literacy**.

> **Supports an experience that should be fun…/…**

> The **players** will be engaged to develop a rich understanding of any situation in order **to fill a gap** between **facts** and **uncertainty**…/…

> By using the toolbox, the players / learners will be able
> - to **understand systems concepts**,
> - to **use systemist attitudes** when considering problem.
> - …/…

> The toolbox can be used by individuals or groups: of all ages, culture and experience as well as **systems scientists and systems practitioners.**

> Through using the toolbox we can help promote and develop the scientific foundations of systems.

> By playing a *SysteMystery game* the learners will be able to reflect on a situation and make improved decisions or judgements.

Playing the Game has three phases:
- a phase of **experience** which would be the story, game, poem, song or explanation of problem or situation;
- a phase of **reflection & analysis** which would be an examination of the experience using the SysteMystery cards;
- a **post analysis** phase where improvements to the SysteMystery framework are considered and fed-back to the repository.

The relevant steps of the Game scenario are:

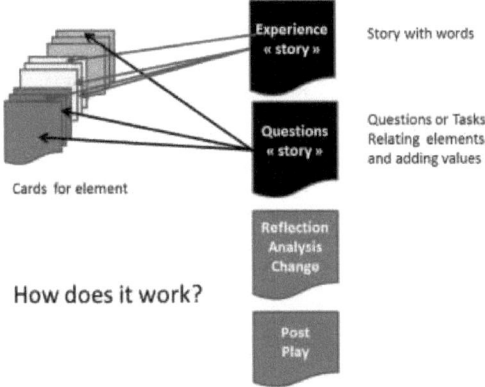

Reflecting on the overall experience, the most compelling aspects of the team's conversation is that can be very difficult for a team to collaborate without having first developed a common vision and mission. This is probably one of the strong messages of the experience with the conversation set-up. In fact the first journey we had to make was the discovery of each other and the plan to build the team through sharing objectives was sadly misinterpreted at the start. As a consequence of the tense emotions, several members of the team on the first day rather behaved as observers rather than full participants. However on a much more positive note, after the first day each of the team members were invited and able to share and suggest insightful contributions.

The platform "SysteMystery" as started in Linz has evolved to reflect the matrix that was designed during the conversation and thus contributes to the Systems Literacy project.

Part 3 – Individual Members' Reflections

Brigitte Daniel Allegro - Reflections

brigitte.daniel.allegro@gmail.com

The Conversation on *"Unity In Diversity – Making the Implicit Explicit"* has been a deep human experience revealing Lights & Shadows of life.

The preparation of the conversation started at the end of ISSS 2015 event in Berlin where I asked Mary Edson if the idea of developing a game to support Systems Thinking training would be a crazy idea for an IFSR conversation. Gary smith agreed to contribute to this adventure. The preparation has matured during several months. Gary and I experimented different ways to get a team to converge on a common understanding of Systems Thinking concepts - *metaphors such as jazz jam or tales (from Jean de La Fontaine who was inspired by Aesop's tales), drawings, exercises of translation of concepts into mother language*. We defined a rough roadmap to engage the team in a learning process (from challenging & updating the *Systems Tree* concepts to the realisation of a tangible prototype of a game, a kind of toolbox). We also had in mind to experiment co-design while developing the prototype.

But three months before the event we still had no member in the team. IFSR Executive Committee helped us to find members. We knew only one person of the team. The journey began altogether a few weeks before Linz: some e-mails were exchanged, some "exercises" done by the team, some useful contributing papers from Gordon and Gerhard allowed to generate some ideas. Gary and I were very busy during the months prior to the conversation and even if we read and appreciated these papers, we did not take time to start a conversation from these seeds. We had a long skype session with Gerhard and a short one with the other members, except with Xijin due to skype problems. This road map has been presented and sent to the whole team before Linz.

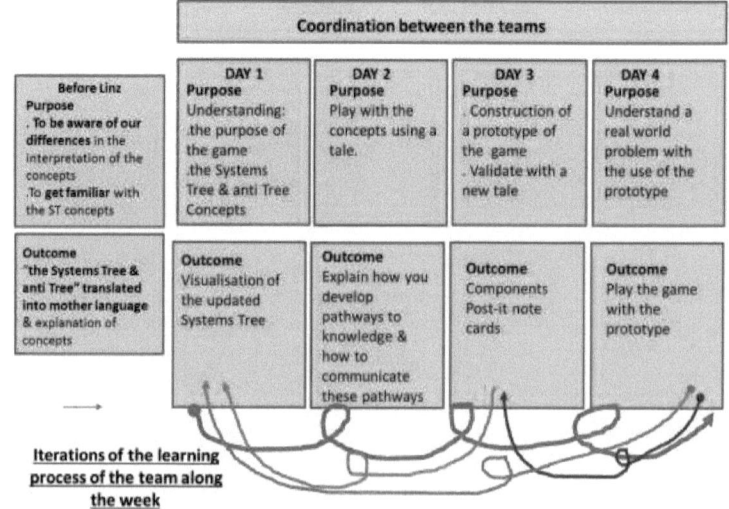

Some word-pairs came to my mind during the week in Linz and may illustrate the "Lights & Shadows" I experienced : (Dream & Reality), (Unity & Diversity), (Inclusion & Exclusion), (Divergence & Convergence), (Synchronisation & De-synchronisation), (Openness & Fixed Mindset), (Slow process & Urgency to produce), (Skip over steps & Slow learning process), (Aggregation & Disintegration), (Leadership & Facilitation), (Tension & Relaxation), (Systems Tree & Anti-tree), (Mutual support & Isolation) etc. These word-pairs reveal some of the difficulties I experienced during this week leading to an accumulation of discomfort.

Some other words came also to my mind during the week in Linz when thinking about the team, Stella, Xijin, Florian, Gordon, Gerhard, Gary and myself. *Warmness, wisdom, patience, stimulation, wealth of ideas, variety of thoughts, richness of cultures, cultural curiosities, support of the team, flexibility, surprises, discoveries, intellectual curiosity, breakthroughs, relationships, mutual support.*

Some more words are still coming to my mind seven months later which may reflect this experience: Unity In Diversity – Making the Implicit Explicit is an art of living.

Gary Robert Smith: Reflections on Linz

Gary.smith@persescomms.com

Memories of events have always been a bit of a problem for me. Generally I have a terrible memory for things that have happened. Concepts and principles tend to stick. Emotional memories tend to stick a bit better.

I remember how this all started. I was at the ISSS Conference 2015 in Berlin and it had been a very memorable and emotional week. My mind was buzzing with concepts like "universal consciousness", principles like "Relational Theory" and how this could form the basis to underpin systems engineering practices. I remember sitting down at breakfast on the last morning and Brigitte, suggesting that we put in a proposal for the IFSR Conversation to the IFSR with the intent to substantiate a game that would teach the concepts of systems thinking. I remember thinking, "that sounds great... but do we really have the time to do this with all of the other crazy stuff we are doing". I remember agreeing "ok, let's do it".

As the months passed and we participated in some of the planning meeting with the other Conversation team leaders, the idea to bridge all of the teams into a goal of starting the development of systems literacy emerged. The concept of a Jazz, both within the game team and across all of the teams also emerged and the idea to create not just a unity, but a harmony from diversity.

From the very start, Brigitte and I shared the same passion and goal to ensure that our team was as diverse as possible - age, culture, gender, profession, hobbies, language. We tried hard to reach out and quickly realised that budget was going to be a constraint, as ever. Despite this we were very pleased when old friends stepped forward to help and new colleagues were found. In the end the diversity of the team was pretty good.

As we got closer to the event, we got in touch with other people who had been thinking about systems thinking and who had lots of experience in delivery systems thinking education. We discovered and rediscovered lots of games that are used to encourage systems thinking.

My thoughts and feelings as we were approaching the conversation were as follows. I was thinking that we did not know exactly what was going to happen, we did not know what the shape of the game would be, but I did have 'some' confidence that something wonderful would emerge. Just before our last skype with the team and before we set out for the EMCSR 2016 Conference in Vienna (a conference traditionally held immediately before the IFSR Conversation), we laid out a framework for the days in terms of key milestones that we wanted to achieve:

- Sharing, playing and visualising the system concepts
- Using the system concepts to analyse stories
- Building the framework for the game
- Using the game to analyse a real world problem

We arrived at the site of the IFSR Conversation in Linz. To be honest I was already quite tired. I have to travel a lot with work and during the week before the EMCSR I had again been away from home. Then having attended the EMCSR just before Linz, I realised that I was missing home, family and was tired, too. Work has also been pretty stressful. I'm working on a transformation project that affects the whole of my company. There has been a lot of argument and debate about the process architecture of our future for which I've been given responsibility but not necessarily the authority to close the debate and declare "the debate is over, this is how it's going to be". The diversity of viewpoints is enormous, a wicked problem at the very least.

Our first meeting with the team in Linz did not go so well. I was honestly dismayed, very surprised and stunned when Gordon and Gerhard did not want to review the objectives for why we were there. It seemed we had stepped immediately into an argument and not a conversation. "Why are these people here if they do not even agree with the objectives?" I wondered. I remember thinking, "why on earth am I here", if it was not for Brigitte, and I remember saying this to her later, "If it was not for you, I would just go home".

I remember Gerhard saying "It's not possible to create a game in four days; this is going to take years". I remember saying "actually I think it is and we have a framework for these four days that is going to allow us to do it." I remember thinking "these guys don't trust us and they don't believe us." (Now on reflection many months afterwards I think this reinforced my determination to deliver)

Recall, my statement at the start of this brief, my memory is not that good but I also distinctly remember Gordon saying "I'm not trying to spoil things" and my reply "I'm sorry but it certainly sounds like it". Thank goodness for Gordon, bless you; this is when you introduced the idea of the "Baron-and-Baroness" plot. This allowed us to at least start to have a reasonable conversation and to get to know each other a little better.

After the plot and lunch, I remember Brigitte suggesting that we try to do some drawings of system concepts. Again I remember the sense of distrust, and it was said, "Do you think this is going to help us to progress?" "Poor Brigitte I thought", I remember saying "Do you think we would suggest this if we didn't think it would? You need to give us some more trust".

I felt that the drawing exercise did help a little in sharing some root concepts and sharing their meaning but this did not complete the work that we had hoped to achieve during the day. I felt tired, depressed and withdrawn by the end. I also felt, maybe wrongly, that several of the team had also been very reticent and withdrawn. Not a good start and it was very difficult to recover.

At the end of the day, during debrief, the highlight for me was when Xijin drew some Chinese characters. I remember thinking that Xijin seemed surprised that we were genuinely interested, but it was clear that we all were.

One day two, Brigitte and I had discussed the idea of doing a roundtable. We had hoped to do it on the first day, but we had lost an hour of the first day due to an unexpected kick off meeting. On reflection we should have gone ahead with this as we had planned, I think it would have helped a lot to share expectations, perspectives and build a common vision.

During the second day we shared some more stories and Xijin shared her translation and explanation of the Chinese characters related to system concepts. By the end of this day, we had agreed what the nature of the game would be in terms of qualities and framework. Its scalability and the idea that it's scaling and tailoring using the concept in relationship to the stories and games already embedded in culture. I remember wondering if everyone shared the understanding of this. I remember presenting this in the systems literacy session.

On the third day we were joined by Peter Tuddenham in the morning. We had some fun with him, getting him to run a round table on the topic of "what can you do to support systems literacy" and then exposing him to the "Baron-and-Baroness" plot. Gordon performed the narration wonderfully, it sounded even more fun this time around.

This is where I messed up and upset Brigitte. With a framework in mind, what was clearly the next step for me in terms of progress was to fill in a matrix of system concepts and related simple questions that could be asked. It is a bit hazy as to what happened and when but instead of getting everyone to work together simply using the systems tree, what I think I did instead was split the team into groups and analyse different sources of potential concepts as contributions to the matrix. I didn't think I was doing anything wrong at the time and I thought this was consistent with the plan as we had agreed that we would introduce the other sources as a way of verifying the content. By the end of the day we had defined a set of questions related to the simple case and identified concepts that were more closely relatable to simple systems. I felt, wrongly or rightly, that we had made good progress but I also felt that it had been really hard work keeping the team on the track of producing a game (for the performance and reflection of systems thinking) that was not the game (a game, song or situation, such as the "Baron-and-Baroness" plot, which is simply the context for the experience).

Day 4, it all went well with a really great result in terms of the game, but went really wrong for Brigitte and I. There was a tension between us; I wasn't sure where this was coming from. I thought it was due to stress and tiredness. I thought perhaps we had a different of opinion on the game not being the game, but this turned out later due to the approach taken on the third day. Did we do a round table on this fourth day? I think we did? Gerhard ran it I think on diversity. Unity and Diversity coming together to form University (Universal harmony came to my mind).

During the morning of that day, Gordon and I finished the word document that described the overview of the game, incorporating the "Baron-and-Baroness" plot as the example. Brigitte and the rest of the team came up with the idea of producing a digital platform. We all then worked pretty quickly in the afternoon to define digital cards and questions for many of the system concepts. Everyone was able to work within the framework and make very strong contributions. Brigitte worked with Gerhard in the evening to finish of the presentation for the next day.

We had accomplished pretty much what we aimed at but the product was not the product I was expecting, it was much better, truly a framework for teaching, developing and practicing Systemry that would be scalable and adaptable to all possible users.

The Linz experience for me was very stressful; the stress being self-imposed as a consequence of the environment that was created at the onset of the conversation. The whole idea of a Conversation I suppose is non-stressful creativity but I guess for me the most important thing in this case was capitalising on skills, experience and diversity of the team during this unique opportunity in order to achieve the end product (and on reflection to prove that, yes indeed, it could be done). For Brigitte and I, this has been a very painful experience for us both, we continue to work together and our partnership is healing for which I am very grateful.

Gordon Dyer: Personal Reflection on Team 2

gordon.dyer@btinternet.com

I was only able to attend the the previous IFSR Conversation in Linz in 2014 via Skype. Successful as that was, there is nothing like being face-to-face conversation, and indeed actually being at a Conversation, for the opportunity to speak with others outside of the team sessions. The 2016 Team 2 experience was especially rewarding as we represented such a rich range of cultures spanning three continents and five different "first languages". I congratulate the non-English speakers on their standard of English which they maintained so well over the five days and hope that they in turn found that experience worthwhile.

Preparation for the conversation had not followed the normal pattern of sharing of input papers, and as a result there was some confusion about the aim. The misunderstanding, which was over what seemed to be an ambitious pre-planned agenda, was not settled until Day 2. The main issue for me was the use of the term "the game" as a basis for teaching systems literacy. This implied to me that a game had already been pre-selected for such a purpose. This was not acceptable from a conversation perspective where progress should only take place on the basis of "designing with others" and not "for others". When it emerged that "the" game was really intended to mean "a" game one focus for my disagreement went away. At that point, as far as I was concerned the team was then potentially in a position to work constructively together. I tried my best to facilitate that by suggesting activities to diffuse tension when this arose through attempts to reintroduce what appeared to be a set agenda. I am grateful to colleagues for taking up such offers. The "Baron-and-Baroness" plot proved to be a surprisingly good catalyst for conversation. I had only previously used the plot for management training, often in a workshop on perception, and my thought that it could be used as a vehicle to draw out key systems concepts was readily adopted by the team. It also met the needs of the team leaders to contribute to the over-arching theme of the conversation of "systems literacy". As well as drawing out systems concepts it helped to develop a list of questions and sample answers to highlight and explore these concepts. Having concept symbols, relevant questions relating to the concept, and sample answers on cards also mapped onto Brigitte's wish to develop a "toolkit". The fact that technology exists to enable Florian to capture all of the same output digitally, and thus to make available on-line, was an important learning point for me.

The group's coming together was also facilitated by Peter Tuddenham's and others' description of the opportunities presented for funding by the US Federal Government for clarifying, defining and educating for systems literacy. This coupled with the growing involvement/interest of INCOSE in conversation and systems education certainly helped me to compromise with my original position and work positively towards a clear outcome which Gary and Brigitte had wanted.

Gerhard Chroust's Retrospective: The Conversation that was not

gerhard.chroust@jku.at

By now I have participated in 12 Fuschl/IFIP Conversations and had all kinds of experience. What I appreciated in all of these meetings was the free-wheeling discussion. The wish and the intention to break out of the stiff rules of paper-presenting conferences and also forcing a team to working to a pre-defined goal.

In 2016 it was different. The official topic of the Team was „Unity in Diversity: Making the Implicit Explicit"

To my surprise the team leaders came with a fixed, rather narrow objective: "Develop a Board Game which supports learning systems thinking" and a tight schedule of work.

Instead of fostering discussion ("diversity") during the preparation phase before the start of the Conversation, they gave us ‚homework', but these contributions were never discussed in the conversation.

A so-called "System Tree" (see above) was introduced beforehand: a graphical representation of many systems concepts. But the system tree was considered to be hewn in stone - discussion was suppressed ("unity"?). One homework was to translate the terms of the systems tree and some of the associated definitions into our mother tongue – but in the conversation it was just ignored – I do not know what the team leaders intended to do with it.

In the opening we were presented with a day-to-day schedule of what we should achieve – with the aim to have a complete card-board Board Game at the end of the conversation.

The basis for the game should be a chosen fable by Aesop (by all means, why by a Greek poet from the 6th century BC from a society which had slaves, where a small minority of men ruled and women had not rights?).

I submitted some ideas about gamification. No, we were expected to work on the 'physical' Board Game. The team leaders even supplied modelling dough, cardboard, scissors, etc.

Gordon and I fought against this straight jacket. With some success.

Fortunately Gordon introduced another story ("Baron-and-Baroness" plot) as the basis. It was very subtle and ambivalent, allowed many interpretations and made us all thinking about some basic questions about responsibility and ethics and Right and Wrong.

As a compromise we agreed to go ahead and discuss the implementation of this plot as a game – and very soon we realized that such a complicated plot cannot really be implemented as a card-board game – it should be supported by computer.

To move along we agreed that we will take the "Baron-and-Baroness" plot as the basis for a real game with some haptic aspects and thus satisfied the intentions of the team leaders. From then on we worked to grind out some of the details, e.g. printed cards for the game-moderator in order to help the participants to express the systemic aspects 'they found'.

The 'elements' of thinking were taken from the Systems Tree – but obviously only a few really matched the "Baron–and-Baroness" plot. We did not discuss whether they were the most essential ones, etc. And we provided (finally!) some hardcopy cards for a moderator of this game.

In total the conversation was very interesting for me, partially because I was able to consider some intricate issues of responsibility, etc. and by observing the group dynamic aspects:

I saw a strong and determined pair of team leaders who initially had just the 'production of a cardboard game' in mind and later were convinced to look at it from a more general viewpoint.

What I missed in the conversation was:

a) Any discussion whether the elements depicted in the Systems Tree were all relevant, whether the hierarchical relationships expressed by the tree structure were adequate, etc.

b) A discussion of the homework we did, its implications, etc.

c) A discussion what types of game would be adequate to teach systemic thinking. The use of prefabricated game-pieces made from modelling dough seemed to me to trivial

d) An analysis what type of system concepts are really emphasized in the "Baron-and-Baroness" plot in comparison to other stories (we also had a short look at an Aesop fable, but did not really discuss its implications)

e) The challenge to see the game as an infrastructure mechanism which would allow DIFFERENT stories to be 'inserted', analyzed and 'gamified'.

f) The concept of "gamification", which is currently discussed in many business areas.

I am still glad that I volunteered to choose this team; I learnt a lot and had very good company. And it was fun – which also is an important aspect in my life. My thanks go to all participants, especially keeping up with critical remarks.

Florian Daniel : Linz Conversation feedback

i.daniel.florian@gmail.com

My participation in the Linz Conversations was a happy coincidence, following a discussion we had with Brigitte and Gary after a meeting had in Paris. We were discussing their project and how to make it happen, and our informal conversation went nicely. Sometime later they invited me to be a member of their team.

While I'm not professionally immersed into an engineering environment, the Conversations appeared to have a few traits familiar to me. This is not primarily professional, usually I'd rather write for a thematic event in a professional environment, that I'm participating in, most of those I've experienced usually involving people with very diverse backgrounds, education, activities, skills and objectives – though it's usually rather around education, digital literacy, software development, collaboration, or ICT policies and public services.

Also non-conferences are the most familiar type of events I'm used to attend or organize myself or with a team, with many variations in forms, from bar camps to world cafés, self-organized events and on/offline community meetings, and other event formats freely derived from them or mixing principles from various event formats. All of these usually come with more or less structured methodologies or principle rules, e.g. "bar camp": self-organized, everyone participates, content and schedule is brought by the attendees.

In these events, the main threats I perceive are:

- Unique communication channel: oral expression comfort heavily depends on the persons' fluency, especially when using a foreign language, and also on very personal cultural habits. Relying only on oral communication usually leads to few people monopolizing the conversation, and might block other participant's expression. Using diverse expression forms, combining writing, drawing and non-spoken reflection times, along with systematic speak turn and strictly respected timeouts are interesting countermeasures.

- Lack of clear topic or objective: self-organisation often leads to unclear objectives, especially if the topic or proposed frame hasn't been initially formulated – braking the initial frame is a common rule, but having a shared starting point, even with diverse or opposite point of views, is a required premise to me.

The preparation in the weeks preceding the actual Linz Conversation week was not easy, as the preparation exercises required some time, which I can afford only from time to time. Following the flow of emails is not easy, but reacting to each of them was almost impossible in real time. I chose to limit my preparation to two main batches, one based on the exercises, the other shortly before going to Linz, with full readings of all the material gathered and transmitted by the team leaders. I really lacked the support of online tools to store and sort the messages and content transmitted by the team members.

At the time of my arrival in Linz, I was supposing that I would mainly meet experienced engineers and academics. That idea was mitigated as the Conversations went on, showcasing much more complex professional and personal pathways. These 2 traits (median age grade + engineering background) were however partly confirmed at the same time, but also very much tempered by the variety of contexts, experiences, twists in life. Globally, there was a lot more diversity than I initially expected both within the participants and within every participant's experiences, which was a very good surprise.

The start of our group was very difficult, as the team leaders were blocked off from the start when they wanted to expose the topic, and how they imagined the proceedings of the week. That preparation work and proposal could only be shared at the very end of the week, and would have been extremely useful as it detailed their preparatory explorations, guesses, proposals, and what the whole week work was about, but Gerhard categorically refused anything coming from the team leaders, based on the dictum that conversations should not be imposed by leaders. In practice, the ones who had taken the most time to prepare the conversations were forbidden to share their ideas by a participant trying to take the leadership over the team, under the reason that they should not be leadership in the group, but also regularly reminding about the deliverables and duties of team leaders.

That particular behaviour was extremely surprising to me, and destabilizing for the team, as it illustrated both the two threats for non-conference I mentioned before, under a double bind strengthened by the coordinating role and anteriority in the organization of the Conversations.

That was even more surprising as besides this particular behaviour he reveals to be a very welcoming, friendly and cultivated person, with insightful feedbacks and stories. I interpreted it as an unconscious kind of defensive or management reflex, but still, that really limited the collective process and I felt we could have gone much farther with more respect to the team leader's work and proportions.

I'll keep up a with the negative points to focus on the outcomes later: methodologies are not solutions, but they sometime help to distribute the word, and can also enable some new outcomes that can be missed otherwise. The opposition to team leader's methodological proposals has been exposed, but the lack of tools for the whole event was striking to me.

As an example, I'm used to take shared notes along with other team participants in real time: this enables people to react simultaneously, in real time, and fosters more rich content than sequential speak turn. Also it provides a way of expression for people who are less comfortable with orality.

Without even discussing the pertinence of enlarging the conversations scope to the wide diversity of participants through services like Twitter and other almost real time communication channels, I lacked the ability to store some resources somewhere online, be able to discuss and comment them, or use collaborative writing services. This remark is not limited to online tools, but most online tools enable real time group collaboration, while offline ones usually tend more to lead by a single person (the one who takes the pen, paper, etc.). They are definitely not a replacement for offline tools, materials, techniques, but they can often augment them by enabling new usages: real time consolidation of content, more collaborative processes, unique entry point for all the resources, etc.

The first evening and following day were spent mainly discovering new people, observing the participant's attitudes and trying to figure out what could be my own contribution to the team and to the whole group. We discussed these issues – among others – in particular with Xijin and Stella.

The start of the first team day was hard, for the formerly exposed reasons, but went better after Gordon suggested to tell a story, actually the "Baron-and-Baroness" plot (p. 42), which took a great place in the next days. That plot, and probably even more the fact that the proposal did not came from a team leader, loosened the initial tension brought by the systematic opposition to them.

Gordon's plot framed a lot the next days – and indeed was a very interesting base. However, we did not really have the opportunity to explore the artistic and creative approaches proposed by the team leaders.

After the first day, the work went better, as the team members learned to know each other and revealed themselves, and tied more as a group. I regretted a little in the first days that there were not many exchanges with the other groups' members: that came progressively, but could be a little more fostered (not sure what would be the best method though). However, this type of event is much better at this (knowing to know each other) than the average similar events, which is a good thing. Staying together in the evening is a good tool for that, but not everyone does. It is also certainly harder for newcomers like myself than for people who participated a few times before (it is always easier to identity a few new people than discovering a whole group at once); a second edition would definitely be a different experience for me.

The diversity of our group revealed different point of views, experiences, stories, ways of embracing complexity and problem solving methods and tools, in various environments, which was enlightening and motivating. Difference is what creates the conversation and the richness of its content, and it was pretty well represented at our small scale. Not everyone agreed on everything, but everyone had the opportunity to express some of their ideas, and that was very nice and useful.

A very good point for the Conversations is the length, and "campus-like" context: it enables deeper understanding of the participant's ideas, positions, experiences, and therefore more intricate exchanges and collaboration patterns, both within the team and the whole group.

I have met there very nice and interesting people, and would reiterate the experience if I were invited to.

However, the difficulty of the exercise, as an independent worker, is to take the time to get there and spend a whole week with my work being put in bracket: it took me more than a month to catch up with my temporarily abandoned work, and of course there is backing from any organization to support the time and expenses spent. It's certainly worth it, but is indeed a blocking issue for potential participants, especially if the organization were looking for more diversity

Maria Stella LOBO: Weaving impressions from the IFSR conversation in Linz

clobo@hucff.ufrj.br

About Systems Literacy ___Enhancing systems literacy means to expand the understanding of the world we live in. From a simple one-sided point of view (tame issues; innocuous solutions) towards a networking of perspectives (wicked issues; complex desirable solutions), there is a long scaling-up way in order to cope with uncertainty and to fill the gaps that surround real problems by means of assumptions, knowledge, solidary practices and creativity.

Somehow, increasing the scale of levels of systems understanding among different groups of human kinds is co-carrying the seeds for the world future – a metaphor for the nurture of the systems tree.

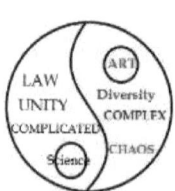

Unity in Diversity:

Any piece of reality you choose to take in your hands has both concepts, intrinsic and simultaneous (synchronous concepts*), depending on the scale (or the level of aggregation) you are considering.

* Synchronous concepts – apparently opposite, always simultaneous, feedback-loop related.

You have a solar system as a unit, and many planets with different physical-chemical characteristics (and biochemical/life possibilities) inside it. You have the planet earth as a unity, and a multitude of continents and cultures inside it. You have Team 2 at the 2016 IFSR Conversation in Linz as a unit amongst other teams, composed of different people, with different ages, backgrounds and cultures, supposed to take advantage of this diversity to create a game to expand the knowledge of core systems concepts.

For creative purposes/solutions, diversity of perspectives is a value itself. [1]The different points

---

[1] In Brazil, the new government ministry team has only men and white people, what has been a target of many criticisms, the image of social backtracking.

of view for responsibility/ culpability seen in the "Baron-and-Baroness" plot is an iconic full of strength introduction to the systems core concept of the stakeholder´s perspective.

For the sake of system´s literacy, metaphors[2] and art facilitate communication among individuals and cultures, by means of mental models. Sometimes, the simple act of translation may operate as a new metaphor, when unexpected understandings may appear. Let´s see an example for a Portuguese speaker listening to the English verb: "to dress". I understand we can dress a wound (cleaning and covering it with a bandage), a salad (with oils and spices), or put clothes on a child (in Portuguese, we do not "dress" salads or wounds). In any of these circumstances, dressing means covering with a specific purpose (cure, taste, protection and beauty). Going further, I could have heard/said a metaphor somewhere: "Increasing systems literacy dresses the world for the future". This may mean making ... A surgical curative to heal noxious environmental problems we face? A flavoured sauce to turn life spicy when depression is already an important public health problem? New clothing to science towards less reductionist problem-solving approaches? Or simply cultivating a field for the future (dress a field, another system tree metaphor). Each new understanding means a diverse mental model, adding new contours and pathways to the group; meta-metaphors.[34] The same happens with art, with new perceptions enlarging any piece of work at multiple dimensions of feelings and understandings.

Playing the game of understanding: describing our auto-organizing process of creation

During the first two, two and a half days, there seemed to have a lack of a glue/bond between the members of the team, associated with three main points of argument:

- Scope: number of concepts to be covered by the game; how to introduce relationships between concepts; scalability and/or hierarchical relationships between concepts.

- Process of creation: there was some criticism towards the prior existence of a schedule for the activities and/or the schedule´s level of flexibility/resilience.

- Model: at first, not all the members were convinced that the system´s tree was the better representation to introduce system´s concepts.

Besides these questions, activities went on, with the introduction of the "Baron-and-Baroness" plot (see Fig. 4 on page XXXX), the drawing of concept pictures, the presentation of videos about games and networking, and the respective areas of knowledge. The introduction of the "Round Table" practice also helped to balance discourses and responsibilities.

In the middle of the third day, we could say the game EMERGED. It was not exactly an A-HA instant, but a moment of collective empathy and doing together (the glue bond) after the second reading of the "Baron-and-Baroness" plot, followed by the activity of filling the matrix (simple→complicated→complex VERSUS concepts → questions → visualization). After the emergence, everybody was aware something new has occurred; some cheeks blurred, other eyes sparkled and smile expressions were visible, with subtle signs of pleasure.[5] From then on, practical discussions just flowed and the game took form:

- From the basic scalability structure to the validation process by feedback loops;

- From the physical package/ card game to the networking media/ digital platform.

In some way, the SYSTEMS TREE model could synthetize and give clues to understand the

---

[2] J L Borges, an Argentinean author, in his book: History of Eternity, defines metaphors as secret sympathies of the concepts.
[3] To be distinguished: as a leverage point or as a dead end.
[4] In Portuguese, we have the metaphor "to dress the hood", that means: identify yourself when someone is talking about a behavior you have or a situation you´ve been involved with.

[5] If we had a theater director inside the team, he/she would easily construct a narrative of body behaviors/patterns through the creative process.

auto-organizing process (although I'm not the best person to represent this graphically, it could be interesting). The first "looking for a glue" days were mainly dedicated to the roots of the tree: the purpose of the game, which components/concepts to work with, how to explore the relationships between them, how different cultural contexts could influence behaviour, and how could ourselves build identity as a team, just to give a few examples. Nevertheless, the team was supposed to act like a system thinker (and succeeded). In the process of building the game, there were lots of reassessments, new perceptions, anticipations, identifications of leverage points that guaranteed the creative flow. Note: nothing would happen without empathy.[6]

"It happens that the *SysteMystery game* is quite different from the proposal."

About the Game[7]: Few questions and Proposals

Two very interesting sentences of our presentation: "It happens that the *SysteMystery game* is not the game". "Reflecting on your attitudes to the game is the game".

Question: Is this a definition of a Meta (second order)-game?

Contributions to SystemsMystery Mind Map

1) Quality of the Game (or Purpose?)

- It is more than a Win-Win game. Everybody gets out of the game richer in knowledge than before entering it; moreover, the collective gain in knowledge is higher than the sum of the parts (Hyper-win, Synergistic-win game?).

2) Purpose of the Game

- Improve Systemic Sensibility

Contributions to Facilitator Notes for playing the "Baron-and-Baroness" plot

1) **Script of the plot:** should we present the characters with letters instead of numbers to avoid the influence of the ordinal sequence in the final choice...? (this was an advice of a psychologist to whom I told the plot) (Two persons to whom I told the story, answered with the order 1-2-3-4-5-6).

2) **Development of the Post Play:** After summarizing the key issues, it lacks something about closing and continuity. Proposing local stories/music/experiences/ problems? Comments about cards/concepts? Depicting cultural obstacles and facilities? Feedback to digital platform/ networking?

The role of ART: we should introduce more art tools inside our game

One of the obstacles for spreading systems literacy is society's aversion to complexity, uncertainty and intersubjectivity. Except in the context of art.

Let's play some music. We have the chord sounds (harmony), melody and rhythm, but each component seems quite incomplete without the other. Harmony without melody has no identity. Playing the same music with different rhythms bring completely different perspectives to it. A group of musical chords may seem more complicated in one song than in another; but join melody and rhythm (not to mention lyrics) and the situation can change completely (increasing lots of complexity to simple harmonies).

If you go to a concert hall to hear a great Mozart's piece, you can look at the stage and see the components (instruments/players) that will interact among them and with other instruments as well (by means of dependencies, influences). The presence of a soloist makes it clear that some hierarchy already exists between instruments. While they are tuning up instruments, you feel that listening to the music itself has an exciting purpose, with different drivers for players and for those who are attending (including us) - In my case, a wonderful birthday gift from Stefan Blachfellner and Mary Edson.

---

[6] Despite any asymmetry of knowledge or language difficulty, the empathy power surpasses all gaps of communication.
[7] Just curiosity → The word game in Portuguese: JOGO, derives from Latin JOCUS or IOCUS, that meant "joke, mockery", and then turned into LUDUS, "game, entertainment, recreation", but the same root LUDUS originated the Portuguese word "ludibriar", that means: deceive, cheat (like the semantic relation between game and gamble).

Reflections from Vienna and Salzburg: Each one has its own history/context that ended to be at that place in that precise moment. Then, comes the conductor and the music begins, like a miracle. You observe patterns, cycles, dynamic states in symphony movements. The more complex the musical arrangement of a perfectly well played orchestra is, the richer issue

Our emotion and the spiritual experience we have (or whatever it is). And all systems concepts are easily found in the description of a musical experience, without any strangeness.

In art, there is no problem with uncertainty. The element of surprise is well received; we look for novelty in art. And we also look for patterns to distinguish one style from another. There is no issue for showing emotions when we face art. Art teaches us that there are many forms to express concepts (beyond words), by using all senses and bodies. It would be very interesting to explore SysteMystery in workshops with artistic groups.

For now, I propose an exercise with the painting: Ship of Fools, by Oskar Laske, 1923, nowadays at Belvedere museum, Vienna.

Finally, subjectivity is not an issue for society in terms of art. When looking to a sculpture, a drawing, a dance or a play, people usually forget the usual "anti-tree" model attitudes and become more flexible to changing, reassessing, looking for alternatives and putting themselves in other people shoes (Another good metaphor for a Portuguese speaker). Imagine a workshop dealing with structure, patterns and behaviours of literary genres!?

That is why art may play a major role in spreading systems literacy. It is a link between the world we live in and the world we should accept. Let´s dress the world with art.

Xijin Tang : Individual reflections on the IFSR Conversation 2016

xjtang@iss.ac.cn

It was my first time to participate in an IFSR Conversation. After having met Professor Gerhard Chroust during the IASCYS International Conference in Chengdu during October 22-26, 2015 and my attending the 1st International Conference on Systems Analysis held in IIASA during November 11-13, 2015, I got invitation from Gerhard about the 2016 IFSR Conversation. Based on my information from Professor Jifa Gu (one of previous IFSR presidents) that IFSR Conversation often last 5-day for free discussions about some dedicated topics from morning to the night, I had hesitation due to my work schedule. Moreover, such kind of conversations are not like normal academic conference where we usually need to give presentations about own research results. Thus if using my research fund to attend such kind of activities, how to report the results?

However, I still managed to attend the Conversation since the original 4 topics were quite interesting. With Professor Gu's information, I suppose I may attend different groups for different topics, to see how the free discussions happen. While I suddenly got emails from Brigitte and just knew I was assigned to Team 2 that was for Unity in Diversity: Making the Implicit Explicit. Brigitte and Gary were team leaders and sent materials for preparation. I was really interesting at this topic, as only from the title I thought this topic was quite close to my research. One of my past research foci is to apply interactive computerized ways to group discussing process, especially to processing group opinions into visualized map (with different structures based on different modeling strategies about opinion representations). Mind map is one kind of tools and adopted by Brigitte while mine is to automatically generate the visualized structures.

From the materials from Brigitte and Gary, later from Gerhard and Mary, I supposed it was quite well prepared discussion. The Guide written by Gordon reminded me about type of group discussions which was summarized into three types of meetings [1] based on Chinese administrative meetings by Professor Gu, i.e. free discussions (just collect diverse opinions), "detailed discussion with deep research" (for research and development and initiate research projects, and for policy/decision making and launch large projects, such as High-speed rail line, new airport, etc. I just thought IFSR Conversation was for free discussions before going to Linz.

I did not finish those homework exercises expected since I did not understand why to do them, such as translation into my language. If I translated the system tree terms into Chinese, but others even did not know even one simple Chinese character, how to evaluate such an action (But the reality changed my mind at Linz). As to art and music related work, I sensed the culture differences or just personal differences, since neither were within my daily attention at all.

I wrote this note after reading all other members' notes toward Team 2 activities. As the event happened almost 8 month ago, really forgot many details. Language is always a big problem for understanding, let alone culture differences. Here just write down some impressive activities in Linz.

1) Opening on Day 1: I got to know background of IFSR Conversation, 3 teams at 2016 Conversation and got to know the names of participants whom I had met before but did not relate to exact persons. I met them on two ISSS events. I once had accompanied Professor Gu to ISSS2010 held at Waterloo, Canada. I serve as an officer of one of IFSR member organizations, the International Society for Knowledge and Systems Sciences (ISKSS) as Secretary General since 2009. University of Hull is one founding organization of ISKSS, thus KSS2011 joined ISSS2011. Since then knowledge and systems science (KSS) has not been removed from ISSS topic list at their conference system (submission process) as I found Gary (Metcalf) and Professor Yoshida (with who I am quite familiar) from JAIST co-organized KSS session at ISSS2015 held in Berlin. Why old faces were of such a big ratio at the Conversation? I myself am for one society normal operation, such an issue actually puzzles me since personally I always hope new and young faces into our ISKSS, such as graduate students.

2) Systems Literacy on Day 1 (17:00-18:00) and Day 2 (18:00-19:00) by Peter Tuddenham.

Due to language and limited understanding, it was difficult for me to get the meaning of Systems Literacy at first. Then I could not understand why a game should be designed at Team 2 with those raw materials brought by Brigitte. Peter introduced his many involved activities, such as Ocean Literacy, etc. I was even more confused with what literacy meant. I bought those books Peter introduced after being back to Beijing. As I read through the long list of organizations especially those universities names, I thought just relating systems literacy as system thinking education was an easier way to understand systems literacy.

The most impressive thing was Peter asked me to write down the Chinese characters of the word 'system'. When I wrote two Chinese characters "系" "统", I heard surprising voices. Stella told me later she felt one sense of structure or framework from both characters. So amazing! The person who first adopted those two Chinese characters was so wise and sure understood both western and Chinese cultures very well. However I did not find evidence that the translation was done by Tsien Hsue-shen whose old house was visited by Professor Metcalf during his October trip to Beijing [2].

3) Team 2's Round Table on Day 2-4

A 2-minute speech at each round really helps to calm down and speak out personal opinions, and useful for system thinking. I did not feel tensions among team leaders at all due to language. While I regard developing one systems game is actually a system practice process. I mean designing or even implementing a game is not a one-shot event but as an iterative process. Then to design a game for systems literacy or systems thinking education itself is one system practice process. Thus Gordon's "Baron and Baroness" story (see Fig. 4 at page XXX) as one game for systems thinking education was a feasible solution. When preparing to teach the Knowledge Management (KM) course for the 1st year graduate students at University of Chinese

Academy of Sciences after backing to Beijing after the Linz Conversation, I had already planned to deliver the ideas that the systems approaches or problem structuring methods could also be played as knowledge generation and management methods during the problem solving process. I thought more things could be taught and discussed among students if using "Baron and Baroness" game at Linz. While it was a pity I did not implement this year; I did not think out a good way to adopt such a game into the fixed scheme.

4) Toolbox for Systems Literacy

I mentioned that we originally endeavored to develop games for people at different ages. I did not understand such an aim, especially could not imagine how to develop systems concept for a 3 year old child. Is it too ambitious or too early ? Systems thinking is somewhat a self-learning and self-disciplined process, where systemic insight may come from personal intuition or drop into one's mind all of a sudden. For modern science and technology, systems thinking may be regarded as one part of a mind model which controls or manages system practice and problem solving process, which can be taught by modern education way. Thus I introduced to use visualized analytical tool to show how group opinions evolving along one process. Again it was a pity that my laptop brought to Linz did not support running the very old version of my designed software 8 years ago.

Finally we were involved into developing a toolbox for Systems Literacy. We just proposed different questions for different kind of problems/contexts. The category of problems is Dave Snowden's Cynefin framework about decision context (simple, complicated, complex and chaotic), which is within the scheme of my KM course . Thus I really preferred to adopt this category, also referred at Brigitte and Gary's booklet about Systems Tree [3]. Other categories were proposed but with no clear professional or academic support or references. Adopting available category accepted and familiar by community is better for future dissemination. Florian quickly provided one application so that we wrote down questions for each category.

Seems the aggregation of all proposed items were our results for the game.

Above all are my current impressive memories toward the Team 2 and all Conversation.

Next are my reflective thinking toward experiences at Linz Conversation.

1) Small Circle issue.

I met old faces who actually let me not feel lonely at Linz and I was so happy to know all members of Team 2 (all new faces to me except Gerhard). I think Team 2 really brings new things to the Conversation. But all around, I am not sure if the Systems Thinking circle is expanding or just staying or shrinking. If Systems Thinking is so useful or valuable, why is the circle so small?

2) Toward Professional or Academics

I am impressed that more professionals (for consulting) were involved in the Linz Conversation. I think Systems Thinking education or training maybe more effective toward professional people instead for graduate students (even for management science and engineering students). At Linz, Brigitte and I had private talks about her experiences, which exhibited she was a successful example of systems thinking training for professionals. I do not know if Professor Gary Metcalf support my view, while I think his half-day exchange at my organisation end of October may help rethink.

3) Toward general systems thinking or domain/field oriented systems thinking/practice

This point is also a consequence of from the above. With requirement from job market, current graduate students often focus on knowledge, technologies or skills which can help them quickly find a satisfying job. Thus I do not open systems thinking course for graduate students, even I do not strongly push doctoral students to read the respective literature, since they never want to read them at all. I just adopt those systems concepts/methods into KM class, teach young students concrete skills, such as computational technologies of visualizing knowledge or personal opinions, social network analysis, etc. Such kind of methods will be quite helpful to acquire the emerging structure of one observed topic (such as one system) even for their future work. Thus instead of delivering systems thinking concepts generally, is it perhaps better to deliver concepts by practical systems? Even we teach creativity and innovation skills with Systems Literacy. We teach system performance evaluation with systems thinking, etc. And more important, quantitative measures (both hard and soft) are necessarily taught or studied toward effectiveness of systems thinking.

4) Large Influence?

At Linz, for the 1st time I got to know the term System Literacy, NGSS, etc. Exchanges with Peter was really interesting and encouraged me to do something. After being back to Beijing, the thoughts were gone soon. In China, some people on systems engineering (SE) sometimes are often quite excited as the top leaders refer the SE term at their open talks for some big issues, e.g. poverty reduction is one systems engineering or air pollution control is one complex systems engineering, etc. After knowing those relevant news, those excited SE people write emails to leaders of Systems Engineering Society of China and urge them to construct SE group and go to the relevant central government offices to provide help. However, normally we know those government offices do not require such direct consultancy at all. Is systems engineering of such a big influences? We here think it is just one excuse the government officer cannot solve the problems or just depict difficulty situations. If SE is so useful, why were 10 years ago those SE people not invited? A better way is to manage to disseminate up-to-date systems engineering or systems thinking to those officials even they have accessed to systems studies during their higher education period. While systems thinking is a lifelong learning and practice. How to provide effective professional training materials and ways is worth systems thinking.

5) Culture or background differences

For eastern people to understand systems thinking, I think language is one of main challenges. I had read one Chinese translation about Checkland's Systems Thinking and Systems Practice more than 20 years ago. At that time I just guessed the translator might be of just philosophy background, so it was very difficult to understand the meaning. Normally I read the English version for better understanding. While it was quite hard and time consuming. That is why graduate students may not want to learn systems thinking at all. Besides, different knowledge background will block some people and lose interests from the start. There are also systems engineering examples and theories in China and other eastern countries. I suppose Gerhard (Chroust) and Gary (Metcalf) have already been familiar with the Dujiangyan Irrigation System after their visits to Chengdu. That system shows greatness of ancient Chinese, while modern systems approaches are also developed. Due to the language gap and culture differences, they are not familiar to western worlds, such as systems intuition [4] proposed by Professor Wang Zhongtuo who has never been at IFSR's formal activities. That is why sometimes Chinese and Japanese systems people come closer, even when we talk about creative and innovation methods. Western culture will sure dominate IFSR Conversation for long, even with eastern people's participation.

Actually this note grows longer and longer as I finally carefully read the finished summary of Team 2. It is not a normal way to reflect my results of attending an academic workshop on conference. It is just my current thinking when looking through those notes I took down at Sankt Magdalena 7 months ago.

References

[1] Gu J F(2001). Metasynthesis, WSR and Consensus. In Wang Z T, et al eds. Proceedings of the 2nd International Symposium on Knowledge and Systems Sciences (KSS2011, Dalian, September 25-27), pp. 12-16, JAIST Press.

[2] http://www.ifsr.org/index.php/systems-science-presentations-tsien-hsue-shen-forum-beijing/

[3] Daniel-Allegro B and Smith G R (2016). Exploring the Branches of the Systems Landscape.

[4] Wang Z T (2003). Systems intuition: Oriental systems thinking style. Journal of Systems Science and Systems Engineering, 12(2): 129-137, June 2003.

Team 2: Gordon Dyer, Xijin Tang, Brigitte Daniel Allegro (Co-Team Leader), Gerhard Chroust, Gary Smith (Co-Team Leader), Maria Stella de Castro Lobo, Florian Daniel (not pictured)

Brigitte presenting the outcomes of Team 2 o the whole group

Lunch time

Andreas Hieronymi, Xijin Tang

Team 3: Systems Research Team: A Foundation for Systems Literacy

Mary Edson, Team Leader, USA – maredson.s3@gmail.com
Pam Buckle Henning, USA – buckle@adelphi.edu
Tim Ferris, United Kingdom - timothy.ferris@cranfield.ac.uk
Andreas Hieronymi, Switzerland- – andreas.hieronymi@unisg.ch
Ray Ison, United Kingdom – ray.ison@open.ac.uk
Gary Metcalf, USA – gmetcalf@interconnectionsllc.com
George Mobus, USA – gmobus@uw.edu
Nam Nguyen, Australia - nam.nguyen@mzsg.com
David Rousseau - david.rousseau@systemsphilosophy.org
Shankar Sankaran, Australia - shankar.sankaran@uts.edu.au
Peter Tuddenham - peter@coexploration.net (guest member)

In this paper, the Systems Research Team (SRT) details the activities and outcomes of the 2016 IFSR Conversation in Linz, Austria. The 2016 SRT includes: Mary Edson (team leader), Pam Buckle Henning, Tim Ferris, Andreas Hieronymi, Ray Ison, Gary Metcalf, George Mobus, Nam Nguyen, David Rousseau, and Shankar Sankaran, with guest team member, Peter Tuddenham, anchoring the endeavor in Systems Literacy. While the 2014 SRT's focus was answering the question, "What distinguishes Systems Research from other types of research?" an internal focus intended to provide grounding for researchers new to the Systems Sciences, the 2016 SRT's focus is on reaching out to a broader community in order to provide a foundation for Systems Literacy. The team's Conversation revolved around the question, "How can Systems Research be in service to Systems Literacy?" The team's discussions were directed into two essential aspects, separate and integrated, of this question. First, Systems Research serves Systems Literacy by providing a credible foundation for the principles and practices of Systems Science and Systems Thinking in both systematic and systemic modes. Second, Systems Research provides a neutral frame for development of ethical applications of those principles and practices.

The SRT recognizes the exigency in providing foundational principles that can be effectively adopted and disseminated through Systems Literacy. The team's narrative begins with an understanding the urgency for application of Systems Sciences and Systems Thinking to critical issues. Systems research, as with other types of research, is typically a slow generation of results; however, the body of knowledge gained through this process can be confidently used to address complexity in timely ways. The criticality of the need for salient approaches to complexity is shown in a graphic representation of some possible trajectories of applying or not applying these Systems principles in practice.

> In her novel, Sense and Sensibility, Jane Austen created characters who primarily embodied sense (which we will understand through the term 'systems literacy') and sensibility. The meanings she ascribed to these terms were: "Sense" …. means good judgment or prudence, and "sensibility" means sensitivity or emotionality (see https://en.wikipedia.org/wiki/Sense_and_Sensibility). Sense and sensibility (or systems literacy and sensibility) can thus be understood through the systemic concept of a duality, a totality.

The choice of how we respond to these issues relates to a process model that can be applied. Through understanding the relationship of the process model to the trajectory, the team directed its focus to developing a MindMap (Eppler, 2006) of eight essential aspects or features of how Systems Research can support Systems Literacy. These include: Systems Science knowledge base, roles and personas, maturity models, role profile, ontology/vocabulary, perspective/framing choice, frameworks, and political ecology. Each of these eight has its own process of unpacking, which was demonstrated to the Conversation participants by delving more deeply into the aspect of knowledge base. The eight relate to unpacking the Systems landscape in a coherent but loosely coupled investment portfolio (economic, social, and relational) for building *systemic sensibility* in such a way as to be dis/aggregated for different audiences. The week's work culminated in a plan for "Looking Ahead," which outlines the intentions of the SRT to continue its activities in support of Systems Literacy in the upcoming months. An example of this continued work is a workshop, "Toward Systems Literacy, the Role of Systems Research," that was conducted at the 60th Meeting of the International Society for the Systems Sciences in Boulder, July 25, 2016. The following sections describe the SRT's Conversation in detail, with some updates and reflections from the workshop.

Introduction: Systems Literacy as the Bridge from Sensibility to Capability

The opening discussion of the SRT meeting aimed to articulate the value of systems literacy, explore ways in which that value can be realized, and reflect on how Systems Research can facilitate this transition. Ray Ison suggested that systems literacy engenders systemic capability in practice, and achieves this by developing innate talents people have (see Figure 1 and discussion further on). The group adopted this view and Ray's diagram is shown redrawn and slightly expanded in Figure 2.

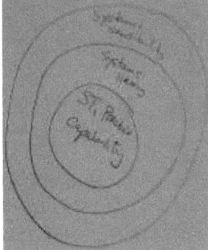

Figure 1. Relationship of Systems Literacy to Systemic Capability in Practice

According to this view, everyone starts out with "systemic sensibility", i.e. an innate, intuitive or tacit appreciation of systemicity in the empirical world. Such a view is theoretically defensible in the light of George Mobus' report that the "language of thought" is systemic, if we combine that finding with the idea from evolutionary epistemology that our cognitive capacities and mental categories are evolutionary adaptations to the intrinsic nature of the world. Systemology formalizes this tacit knowledge, so that education in Systemology provides persons with clear concepts and a common language that gives them the capability to articulate and reflect on this innate sensibility, and act on it in a considered way.

Systems literacy therefore not only empowers people individually but can connect people to communities of practice in which their sensibility can be expressed as a responsible and effective capability. Systemic capability is then enacted in terms of various roles systems literate persons can fulfill as they apply systems knowledge (see Figure 2).

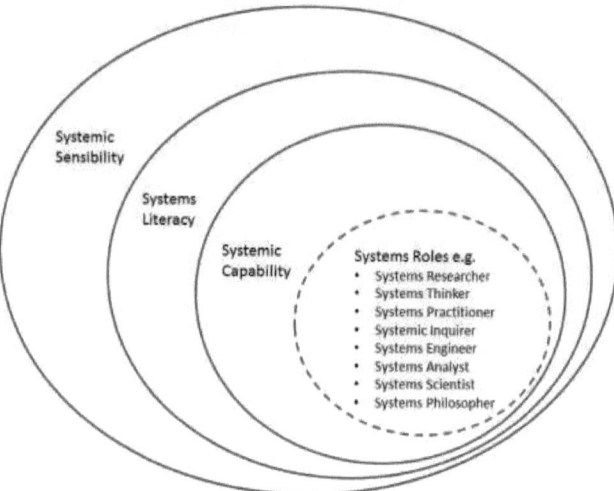

Figure 2. Systems Literacy Refines Systemic Sensibility to become Systemic Capability

The extended version of Ray's diagram shows systems roles as examples of ways in which systemic capability can be enacted. The dotted boundary around the roles serves as a reminder that the roles are not fixed designations but that the same person can fulfil different roles at different times or in different contexts, and that the roles also have some overlaps with each other and roles from other disciplines in terms of their profiles (although there are roles concerned with developing and promoting Systemology per se, the roles typically involve applying systems knowledge in the context of specialized problems, concerns or intents).

The team felt that this framing of systems education as nurturing and empowering a natural talent that is of evolutionary significance is compelling, and a simple diagram like this and the basic narrative that goes with it can serve as an accessible and persuasive introduction to the importance of systems education and the need for investment towards wider systems literacy.

Exigency of Systems Research to Systems Literacy

The necessity for Systems approaches to address larger issues and problems informed much of the Conversation, as the limitations of traditional approaches have been realized. Nam Nguyen shared the following graphic of this trajectory (Figure 3), emphasizing the urgency for putting these approaches into practice (*Note: Colors of "Red Curve" and "Green Curve"* do not carry any meaning except for distinction to illustrate "The Great Transformation21").

Economies and societies are going through a Great Transformation. We have been going through the red curve for a long time with the existing foundations. There is another curve (the green curve) with foundations of future existence.

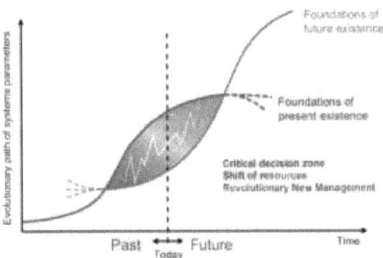

Figure 3. The Great Transformation21 (from the Old to a New World) from Malik (2016) at http://www.malik-management.com/en.

There is a universal pattern of transformational change. It is the particular case of substitution, also called creative destruction. However, growth can go on, but it changes direction. While the Old World is still strongly growing (symbolized by the red curve), a New World is already emerging – slowly and often unnoticed or neglected (symbolized by the green curve). It will substitute the Old World. Examples are the horse cart and the automobile; chemical photography and digital image processing. For long term growth and prosperity, one needs to get onto the green curve on time or face the consequences, anticipated and unanticipated. While in earlier times, societal revolutions were induced by technological innovations, today social technology of system-cybernetic management will revolutionize the functioning of companies, societal organisations and whole countries (Malik, 2016).

The overlap area is a critical zone in which 3 decisions need to be made:

- Keep going on the red curve for as long as possible
- Providing resources to move from the red curve to the green curve
- Getting on the green curve

In order to do the right things today, one needs to know the patterns of change – and recognize them. For us, as individual systems scientists/scholars and also, collectively, as the systems society, it is critical to find ways to move ourselves and the systems field, together with systems research and system literacy, from the red curve to the green curve.

Process Model

Andreas Hieronymi led the co-creation of a visual process model that provides an overview of the role of systems research for the advancement of systems literacy. The following thoughts represent aspects of what the SRT discussed over the week in Linz. We asked ourselves, "Why do we care about systems science, systems literacy and systems approaches?" The purpose is not just about increasing the number of systems books and papers, but finally about the changes we want to see in the world. But how can we bridge the perceived gap between academic knowledge and real-world practice? What are the necessary intermediary factors from insight to impact? The following process model (Figure 4) tries to capture this and consists of five main variables/factors (or pillars) that are linked through a sixth one. In one long sentence we can connect all these aspects as follows: A "high quality of systems knowledge" (pillar one) enables "systems researchers" (pillar two) to gain influence in "supporting organizations" (pillar three) and through them to better enable "systems thinking and acting of individuals and groups" (pillar four) what may lead to more "quality in dealing with complex challenges" (pillar five) and produce "reports and case studies" (sixth factor) that finally feeds back into improving the "systems knowledge base" (pillar one).

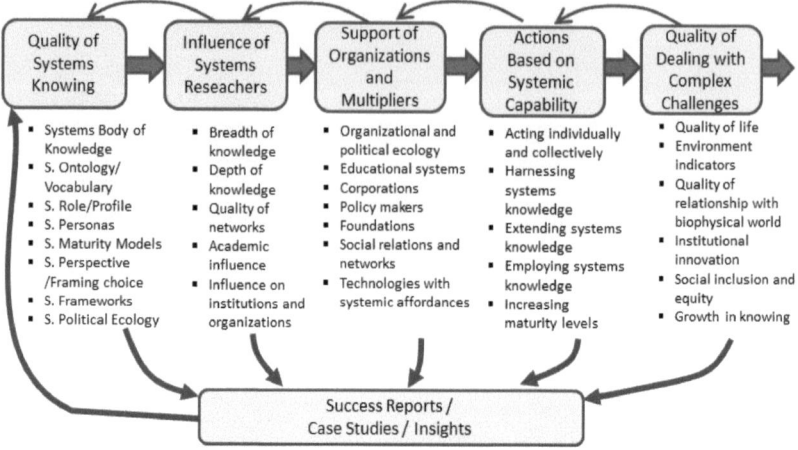

Figure 4. Towards systems literacy – The role of systems research

Systems Analysis – Future Potentials

George Mobus shared his observation that the process started here, at the Conversation, essentially a kind of agile method for finding a set of seed ideas, has provided an excellent beginning for a more rigorous top-down systems analysis. Here is a sense of what we are working on and toward.

The SRT is *acting as a process to generate a process*, i.e. to develop a framework for the production of a set of guiding principles, including possible structures to be employed, for the doing of systems research. The intent of this effort is that by doing so future systems researchers (in different roles such as pure or applied research) will contribute to a common framework in which the other sciences (natural and social alike) can operate to enhance and increase the systemicity of their work. The objective includes a broader application of systems literacy that goes beyond just doing science to the whole of social thinking and doing. The work started here must eventually be witnessed succeeding as social norms in thinking through complex problems (e.g. political)

and move from linear, isolated conceptualization to the systems point of view.

To that end the team identified eight believably critical factors or components that form the structural aspects of the hoped for process. As mentioned, one of these, the body of knowledge of a scientific process (what can be considered "normal" science) was further unpacked by David who had already given (with J. Billingham, J. Wilby, and S. Blachfellner) a great deal of careful thought to what the knowledge base would look like structurally and functionally. This unpacking procedure can be seen as an essentially top-down systems analysis or deconstruction of the parts without losing track of the connections. The same kind of unpacking is needed with the other identified factors. The matter of "vocabulary" will be tabled, but it could be treated as a need for a full language of systems, something George has been working on for several years.

With this proposal, we now have a five-part projection model of what effects we should be looking for as the "product" if our to-be-invented process is conveyed to the systems science research world and hence to the science and social world beyond. While we have referred to this as a Process Model, it may also be characterized as an evolutionary transformation model. This is because what will follow in the long run is not under our, or the systems scientists', or the disciplinary scientists' direct control; it is only under our influence if we do a good job in communicating its value for application in other fields.

George proposed the application of a systems analysis (Mobus, 2015) to what we have so far in order to better identify the actual processes that will produce the actual products and resource inputs needed. He had previously done this kind of analysis to a small degree and will be sharing that work incorporated into a larger systems analysis of what the team is doing and following the longer term societal transformation progression.

Through an iterative process of feedback exchanged with the team, the SRT in essence becomes the "users" (actors or agents) thus capturing the real needs of the users. In other words, the members of the SRT are not merely attempting to be objective observers but participants in the systems in which they research, possibly agents of change and transformation.

Eight Critical Factors

After identifying eight, believably critical factors or components that form the structural aspects of the hoped for process our team decided to explore these further. After debating about whether to use textual forms or visual forms, it was agreed that we prepare a list and then create a mind map for each factor. As shown in the Process Model, the list of eight factors we compiled is as given in Table 1 below.

Table 1. Eight Critical Factors of the Systems Landscape

	Systems Landscape Critical Factors
1	Systems Body of Knowledge
2	Systems Ontology/Vocabulary
3	Systems Role/Profile
4	Systems Personas
5	Maturity Models
6	Systems Perspective/Framing Choice
7	Systems Frameworks
8	Systems Political Ecology

Note: the "Maturity Models" factor relates to three identified aspects: Maturity Models of the Systems Roles, Maturity Models of the Systems Body of Knowledge, and Maturity Models of the Systems Field as a whole.

The team then worked on drawing a mind map of the critical factors (or ways of knowing) and developed separate mind maps of each of these factors.

Using these mind maps and the preceding discussions during the week it is possible to briefly characterize each factor and the relationships between them in the following way.

The **Systems Body of Knowledge** enables the activities involved in expressing systemic capabilities, and it consists of data, methods, methodologies and theories (more detail on this is given further below). This body of knowledge is grounded in a **Systems Ontology/Vocabulary** that captures the core concepts and key terms needed to characterize and explain the kinds and natures of systems, and to articulate assumptions about the fundamental constituents or 'building blocks' of systems. The structure of the systems body of knowledge is akin to that of other scientific bodies of knowledge, and this makes it possible to construct a **'Systems Body of Knowledge Maturity Model'** which can be used to identify key gaps for research attention (more on this further below)

The knowledge base is applied under the guidance of **Systems Perspectives** and **Systems Frameworks**. A **'Systems Perspective'** reflects the fundamental assumptions that are made in systemic undertakings. This involves components of the systems worldview such as a systems ontology (assumptions about the kinds and components of systems), a systems metaphysics (assumptions about the nature of systemic entities) and a systems epistemology (assumptions about the nature and possibility of knowledge about systems). These aspects of the systems perspective condition how systems terms are interpreted (which meanings are applied), and what is framed as a problem or research question in relation to a particular presented scenario. An important aspect of the systems perspective is that it is reflective and reflexive, that is, it is an express aim of systemic undertakings to make explicit the assumptions that underlie perspectives, to critically reflect on how they condition perceptions and possibilities, and to consider the viability of alternative assumptions. It is by critical reflection on such alternatives that alternative **'Framing Choices'** are identified for a given scenario, enabling selections to be made that are appropriate for the given scenario and context rather than having the perspective set a priori. A framing choice therefore represents a systems perspective that is tailored for the specific situation. **'Systems Frameworks'** then formalize how to use a given framing choice to select systems methodologies as appropriate for use a given situation, problem or context, and guide how the methodology and its outcomes are interpreted in that specific case.

The enactment of the knowledge base under the guidance of perspectives and frameworks are executed by individuals that fulfil certain **Systems Roles**, e.g. Systems Researcher, Systems Thinker, Systems Practitioner, Systemic Inquirer, Systems Engineer, Systems Analyst, Systems Scientist, Systems Philosopher. These roles reflect kinds of intentional context in which the person is working, for example exploration, theory or method development, innovation, design, consulting, etc., and each role is identified in terms of kinds of actions that can be performed in different contexts. Each systems role represents some way of being involved in the transdisciplinary activity scope of Systemology, but usually involves systems knowledge combined with some other field of specialized interest, in order to address some specialized question, problem or intention.

Each role can be characterized in terms of a **'Role Profile'**. The role profile matches the technical demands on that role (the kinds of issues/situations the person must be able to deal with) to a range of systems knowledge elements and personal qualities (e.g. adaptability, neutrality) needed for such activity. Each role profile can be further specified in terms of the level of competency required in each element of the systems knowledge base and each kind of personal quality, and this makes it possible to frame **'Systems Role Maturity Models'** which can be used to frame training plans for specific roles, and to assess/certify individuals in terms of their systemic competency for a certain role.

In order to identify the kinds of people who are suitable to fulfill specific roles, one can define a **'Systems Persona'** for each kind of role. A persona is an idealized version of a person that might enact a given role, identifying typical social, psychological, educational, domestic and demographic factors. A persona specification makes it easier to plan recruitment and training, and to anticipate how roles might be acted out in different contexts.

The roles fulfilled by Systemologists are executed within a wider **'Political Ecosystem'** that constrains and enables the potential of Systemologists, via competition with other disciplines for access to respect, acceptance, research funding, student recruitment, inclusion in reviews, consultations and calls for tenders/proposals, etc. Operations within this wider ecosystem is dependent on a special kind of disciplinary role, that of representing the discipline in a context of competition and cooperation with other disciplines and institutions. Every discipline has such a role. In the case of Systemology this requires persons with knowledge of both the scope and depth of the systems landscape and knowledge of the political context in which Systemology has to succeed. Within this political ecosystem credibility is a major leverage point, and this was identified in discussions as an important point to focus on. This was included in the major process overview (see Fig. 4) as involving **'Success Reports'**, **'Case Studies'** and **'Insights'** arising from the systems approach. These items might be treated as data included in the knowledge base of Systemology, but they represent key content for defending the credibility and potential of Systemology in the political ecosystem in which Systemology is an actor. The field as a whole can be assessed in terms of a **'Systems Field Maturity Model'** that can be used to identify areas that need attention to improve the adoption of and support for Systemology as a valuable discipline.

All of these 'critical factors' have to be taken into consideration when working to establish Systemology as a valued and powerful contributor to how academia and industry moves forward in trying to establish a world that is sustainable, resilient, evolvable and, most importantly, fair to all stakeholders.

As an example, in the team discussion the first factor, 'Systems Body of Knowledge', was elaborated as shown in Figure 5.

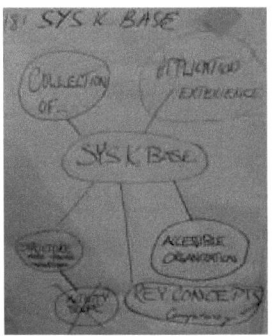

Figure 5. Systems Body of Knowledge mind map of possible elements

In relation to this component David Rousseau then showed us how we can use the work he and others recently did to elaborate further the content on this poster (Figure 5). This could be repeated for all the eight Critical Factors, which could then be used to attract people to invest time and resources for further development.

Knowledge Base of a Discipline

David showed a generic way of modelling the structure of the knowledge base of a discipline. This model was developed by the General Systems Transdisciplinarity team, but it is suitable as a basis for the sort of direction the SRT is aiming at in terms of developing views on the components of the Systems Landscape, as we discussed in the SRT during the week. Three important things should be noted at the outset.

First, the building up of the knowledge base depends on factors that are not part of the knowledge base per se but originate in the discipline's guidance framework. This includes the definition of the subject of interest for the discipline (creating an empirical boundary for the discipline) and a technical vocabulary (which, like the empirical boundary, can be interpreted differentially based on worldviews of individual scientists). Second, the basic knowledge base model is fairly simple, making the model easy to apply. It shows that the knowledge base consists of data, three kinds of theories and also methodologies (with all these terms very broadly construed). This provides a framework for

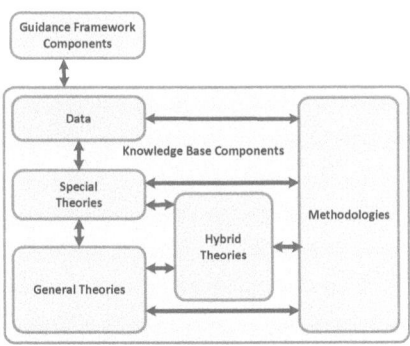

elaboration as shown in Figure 6.

Figure 6. The structure of a Knowledge Base (adapted from Rousseau et al., 2016, Figure 9)

Third, the knowledge base of any discipline is typically developed by working through a set of structured questions about the disciplinary subject, namely what are the subject entities like, how do they work, how do they come about, and why some types and designs do not appear or persist. At each stage we develop descriptions and theories that can support the development of methodologies. The questions address systemic issues of increasing sophistication - complexity ("what are entities like?"), machine models ("how does it work?"), developmental models ("how do complex individuals come about?") evolutionary models ("how do diverse kinds come about?") and eventually holistic models ("why do only some types appear or persist?"), as shown in Figure 7.

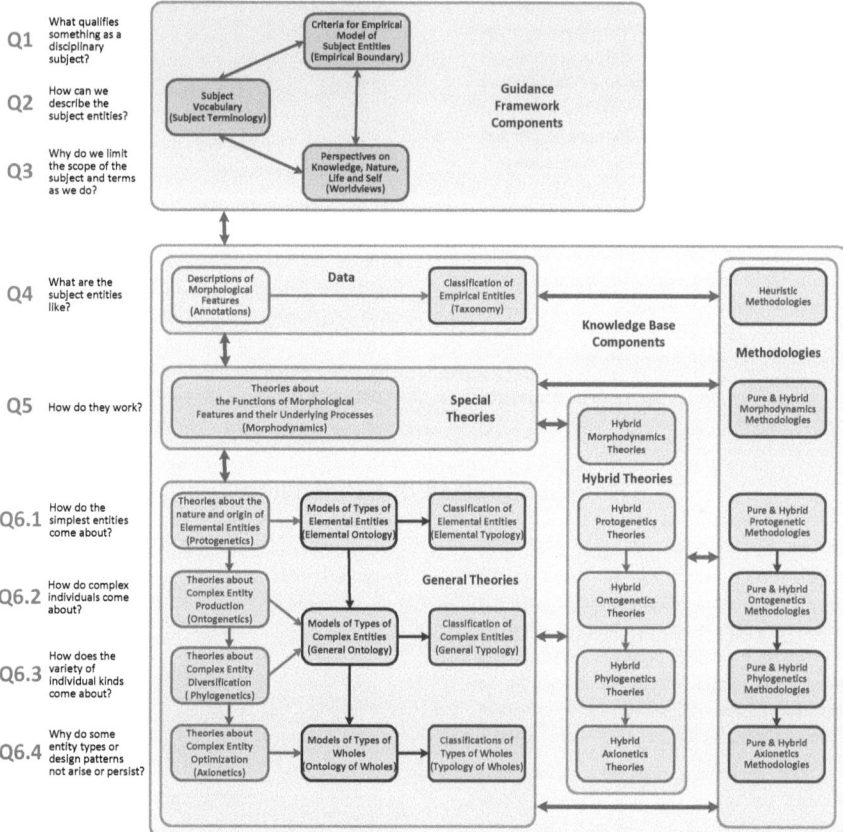

Figure 7. Description and Theory Development through Structured Questions (Rousseau et al., 2016, Figure 9)

Such a model of the knowledge base of the systems field could have multiple uses within the "portfolio" envisioned by the SRT. First, it can be used to make an inventory of current knowledge holdings, showing the scope of present data, theories and models, putting existing work into context and revealing significant gaps. Second, the structure of the knowledge base can be used to index the disciplinary knowledge, making it accessible to systems researchers in a principled way. Third, because the structure reflects work of increasing sophistication due to the progression of inquiry-driving questions, this can be used as the beginnings of a framework for a maturity model of the systems knowledge base. Fourth, because it provides an overview of the available or potential knowledge it can contribute to defining the resources available or needed for performing different kinds of roles within the scope of systems research and practice.

This kind of model can therefore be useful in the context of several of the components of the "investment portfolio' the SRT discussed as a framework for guiding activities that would make progress towards achieving systemic literacy and sensibility in the broader community.

Systems Landscape and Systemic Sensibilities

Ray urged the team to frame the next steps of the contribution of the SRT (or rebranded as the 'Landscape of Systems Knowing Inquiry') as we devised a 'first-cut' model (Figure 4 and Table 1) of an 'investment portfolio' as a device to aid on-going inquiry by us, as well as a means to organize and report on our work and that of other groups committed to supporting transitions to systemic literacy (systemic capability + [systems science + systems thinking in practice or STiP]) (Blackmore, C., Reynolds, M., Ison, R. & Lane, A., 2015).

We understand investment to include financial, individual, intellectual, group, organizational, philanthropic, among other characteristics or attributes, and the 'portfolio' to be designed drawing on concepts of self-organisation, open-source protocols, and easy refinement for different purposes/investors. As outlined earlier we identified eight elements of a possible system to enhance the quality of systems knowing, though the possible systemic relations among these eight are yet to be established, understood and articulated (e.g. there may need to be more or fewer). We suggest that in a 'first-cut' portfolio design each of these eight elements needs to utilize/complete the following template:

- What are the characteristics of the element?
- Why is it important?
- What is a story (narrative) or case study about it - of need, failure, success, etc.?
- Suggest possible 'investment' agendas or pathways - who; how; when?

Perhaps this template needs to be completed also for the outer 'system' in Figure 4 - hence the question mark? Monitoring and evaluation systems against agreed, yet adaptable, measures of performance are needed 'in service' of moving towards systemic literacy. Controlling action will also be needed. These 'systems' will also require a conducive institutional/organizational platform from which to operate and thrive.

Shadow Side of Systems - Systems Ethics

Tim Ferris suggested that Systems Literacy could benefit from looking at the ethics of Systems Research and in Systems Practice and some of its nascent assumptions. There is general agreement among scholars and practitioners interested in systems science and systemic methods that using systemic perspectives will enable them to produce better results in their work than they would achieve if they were to continue to use the discipline perspective approaches to their work that traditionally would have been applied. The improvement that they perceive achieving through the use of systemic perspectives results from producing data/findings reflecting a more complete vision of the situation which enables more complete understanding of the interaction between the aspects of the situation and reducing unintended consequences, and the knowledge to deal with the emergent effects more effectively through better understanding of what they reflect about the situation. This aspect of improvement in work approached systemically improves the results achieved, so the word "good" is appropriate to reflect that the results of work done systemically are more likely to match the actor's intent. That is, these results are "good" from the perspective of the actor intervening in the situation.

In the rhetoric of some systems researchers or practitioners the idea of "good" to describe the results is conflated with the idea of moral goodness, leading to the suggestion that results achieved through systemic work are morally better than would otherwise be achieved, and thus a suggestion that systemic approaches are inherently benevolent and good (Mary drew the team's attention to the notion of " benevolent bias" in the history of the systems sciences). This assumption is not justified since the systems science and methods are, like any other knowledge and methods developed through any approach, morally neutral. The knowledge and methods describe the world and potential ways of acting in the world, with the possibility of providing understanding and prediction in situations of interest to a user of the knowledge and methods. The person using the knowledge and methods constructs their desired learning or intervention outcome based on their own motivation which is developed from their underlying belief structure. The effect is that the knowledge and methods may be used for a variety of purposes, some of which may harm some people or the environment.

As a result systems research and practice must be understood as morally neutral, with potential to be used for good and ill, and therefore in developing systems knowledge, or in the rhetoric of discussing systems and systemic approaches to engagement with the world, it is necessary to avoid the assumption of moral desirability of systemic perspectives, and also to discuss systemic approaches in a way that explicitly recognizes where the moral judgement of the systems practitioner or researcher will impact the choices made.

Looking Ahead and Moving Forward

The SRT left the 2016 Conversation in Linz with two commitments and an invitation. A valuable framework (i.e. the "investment portfolio") has been created, but it needs to be further refined and explored. A summary of what has been accomplished has been created for this contribution to the Proceedings of the Conversation. Beyond this, team members need to decide whether the work is worth additional investments of time and energy. The first commitment was for a team discussion in June, after team members would have time for additional, post-Conversation reflection. This meeting occurred and substantially set the stage for the second commitment. The second commitment was a presentation for the ISSS 2016 Conference in Boulder, CO. That presentation was redesigned into a workshop titled, "Toward Systems Literacy, the Role of Systems Research," that was conducted at the 60th Meeting of the International Society for the Systems Sciences in Boulder, on July 25, 2016. The team redesigned the presentation as a workshop to invite greater participation and feedback from the Systems Community. The workshop resulted in expansion of ideas about Systems Research in support of Systems Literacy, in response to the question, "What does Systems Literacy need from Systems Research?"(Figures 8, 9, and 10).

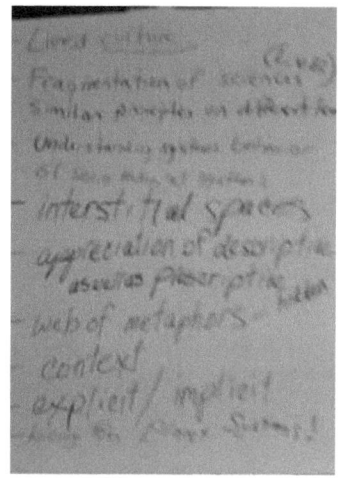

Figure 8. Systems Research/Systems Literacy Workshop Discussion 1

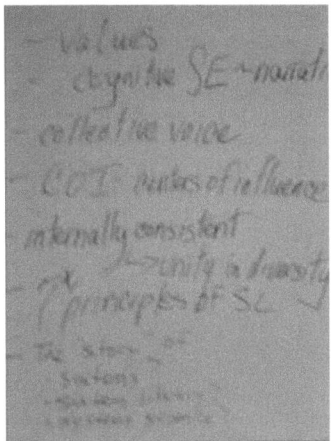

Figure 9. Systems Research/Systems Literacy Workshop Discussion 2

Since the workshop at the ISSS meeting in Boulder, the SRT has developed sub-teams to address different aspects of this project and those teams will continue the work going forward. Perhaps the one of the biggest insights from the workshop was invocation by participants of a guiding principle of *elegance* in our approach to Systems Research in service to Systems Literacy, especially in the light of complexity. The invitation remains open for others to join the sub-teams, especially those who find the initial work to be sufficiently compelling to help in its further development. The true value of the portfolio will be demonstrated by the additional investment that it draws from the Systems Community and beyond.

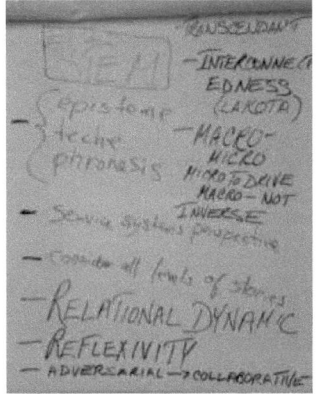

Figure 10. Systems Research/Systems Literacy Workshop Discussion 3

Conclusions and Recommendations

The SRT's Conversation focused on the question, "How can Systems Research be in service to Systems Literacy?" To reiterate, discussions were coalesced into two essential aspects. First, Systems Research serves Systems Literacy by providing a credible foundation for the principles and practices of Systems Science and Systems Thinking in both systematic and systemic ways. Second, Systems Research provides an impartial, dispassionate frame for development of ethical applications of those principles and practices.

In the team's view, successful programs in Systems Literacy will be grounded in Systems Research encompassing: 1.) a *history* of systems thinking (context, sources, and development of key ideas – principles expressed in clear language); 2.) *literature* of systems (a canon of essential theory, results of practice, and criticism); and 3) *transdisciplinarity* (shared relations and effects of systems sciences with other disciplines). The SRT's role is to foster the relationship between these aspects of Systems Research with Systems Literacy in timely and relevant ways.

References:

Blackmore, C., Reynolds, M., Ison, R. & Lane, A. (2015). Embedding sustainability through systems thinking in practice: some experiences from the Open University. In: Wyness, Lynne ed. *Education for Sustainable Development Pedagogy: Criticality, Creativity, and Collaboration*. PedRIO occasional papers (8). Plymouth University: Pedagogic Research Institute and Observatory (PedRIO), 32–35.

Eppler, M. J. (2006). A comparison between concept maps, mind maps, conceptual diagrams, and visual metaphors as complementary tools for knowledge construction and sharing. *Information Visualization*, 5, 202-210.

Malik, F. (2016). *Navigating Into The Unknown. A New Way for Management, Governance and Leadership*. Campus: Frankfurt am Main/New York.

Mobus, G. E., & Kalton, M. C. (2015). *Principles of systems science*. New York, NY: Springer.

Rousseau, D., Billingham, J., Wilby, J. M., & Blachfellner, S. (2016). In Search of General Systems Theory. *Systema*, 4(1) *Special Issue – General Systems Transdisciplinarity* : 76-99 .

Shankar Sankaran presenting the results of team 3

Toward a System of Systems Science Research & Education
(George Mobus)

Abstract

This paper presents some personal reflections on the Systems Research Team Conversation in Linz, Austria, April 2016. As this was my first meeting with the team and in the format of the Conversation I spent much of my time observing, absorbing, and cogitating on the thoughts of my colleagues. It was one of the most rewarding intellectual experiences of my life and the objective of the team fit perfectly with my own concerns regarding the future of systems science, SS research, and its potential impact on society. I have felt for a long time that the future success of all of the sciences and, indeed, the human social experiment, hinges on a broad and deep grasp of systems science and an approach to understanding the world from a systems perspective.

The SRT is attempting to define a process whereby systems science (or systemology), and a portfolio of systems research methods, tools, and techniques might be disseminated to provide support for a range of researchers and educators in order to raise the level of systems knowing (systems sensibility, systems thinking, and systems 'doing') in multiple sectors of society. The overall premise is that if systems science were better understood generally, and if researchers and educators, specifically, had more refined understanding of how systemicity affects the quality of knowledge they produce, then it would become more feasible to tackle and solve extremely important (even existential) problems. Ultimately, I believe that the route to a sustainable human social system will depend on systems understanding and methods such as systems analysis, modeling, and design.

The week in Linz has helped me solidify some of the thoughts that I had prior. This report will attempt to explain how those thoughts have emerged in more clarity as a result of the Conversation. The more evolved thoughts are no longer mine, but belong to the group and other systems scientists with whom I have since collaborated.

The Status of Systems Science in the Social Milieu

Almost every scientific discipline, both natural and social, has a sub-discipline with the term 'system' in it. For example, there is systems ecology, systems biology, systems sociology, etc. All of these sub-disciplines have turned to advanced modeling and, often, interdisciplinary approaches to understanding their subjects. I am, myself, aligned with a new branch of economics, called biophysical economics, which while not using the word systems in its name is a derivative based on the systems approach used by Howard T. Odum in systems ecology. The concept of systems (or systemness or systemicity) has pervaded much thinking in the sciences as they have tackled complexities and cross-disciplinary issues discovered in the disciplines. There is a tacit recognition that issues of complexity and the need for multi-disciplinary approaches are related to how phenomena are organized in systemic ways, hence the need to think about them systemically.

Ironically, even with this recognition, the various systems-related science approaches have generally been limited to only a few aspects of the totality of systems science theory. They are, in my opinion, only weak approaches to systems and so do not benefit from a more holistic conceptualization of systemness. Specifically, each "systems <your science name here>" explores limited subsets of the full power of a general systems theory and methodologies that use that theory to fully explicate phenomena.

The current situation in systems science seems to be that various sub-disciplines, such as information theory, complexity theory, cybernetics, etc. have, themselves, become silos of research and development with limited cross reference to each other. The idea of a unified systems science has been lost in the attempt to gain legitimacy for each sub-discipline in its own right. There are very few academic departments devoted to general systems science and those that exist are having existential crises of their own in many cases (according to Wayne Wakeland, Chairman of the Systems Science PhD program at Portland State University, personal communication). In Thus there are few PhD granting programs for systems science. And once a newly minted PhD graduate is hired they must vigorously pursue tenure and promotion, which comes from publishing in prestigious disciplinary journals. The nature of our (USA) higher education, PhD production system has helped to drive a wedge between elements of a general systems science.

Then there is the simple fact that very many people tend to have particular interests and talents, leading individuals to pursue those interests in more specialized areas. The systems science field today is still broken into a number of professional societies that focus on a particular view of systemness.

Finally, I have noticed another interesting phenomenon among many systems people. I apologize in advance for possibly over-generalizing – this isn't meant as an indictment of any kind, merely an observation of a phenomenon that impacts the potential to integrate the various aspects of systems science. There seems to be a tendency to fixate on the work of one or another of the original founders of systems science. I, of course, think it important to recognize the accomplishments of the founders. They brought incredible insights into the view of us mere mortals! However, I suspect there is more than just effort to 'build on their work' in some instances. Rather there seems, to me, a motivation to place their work as central to the whole program of systems science, to try to explain all systemness based on this work. For many years I have been thinking, in contrast, that all of this foundational work needs to be integrated into a whole picture. This was actually part of my motivation in writing "Principles of Systems Science" with Mike Kalton. I felt it was long past due to re-integrate the various "aspects" of systems science as a basis for understanding all phenomena. This sentiment was expressed by numerous of the founding thinkers themselves so I hope this idea can begin to influence our current generation to work toward that end.

My Thinking Stimulated

During the week at Linz I had a chance to listen to some incredibly excellent thinking that seemed to me to be in accord with the idea that there really is a unified concept of systemness, and that, furthermore, this concept could be the basis for increasing the power of the disciplinary sciences in understanding phenomena as well as those working in research in systems science directly (what David Rousseau calls systemology). We also spent time considering how our work might support the increase in systems literacy generally. In academia the common idea is that good teaching is bolstered by good (and up-to-date) research. So the link seems natural enough.

In the year prior to the Conversation I had already been working on a book project that was meant to be a sequel to my "Principles" book;

working title "Understanding Complex Systems: Analysis, Modeling, and Design." In this book I am developing several concepts that will solidify the approaches to understanding systems. First among these has been a more comprehensive formal definition of systems, extending concepts introduced by George Klir. I presented some of these at ISSS-2016. The second piece I was developing was a formal language, derived from the definition, which could be used to describe any kind of system. I had started with the lexicons and syntax of existing modeling languages such as system dynamics (SD) and had already derived extensions, e.g. delineating flows into matter, energy, and messages, explicitly, in order to develop more realistic models. After Linz I realized that the purpose of a system language was not just to do modeling, but rather to provide an extensible way to describe all systems. Modeling always involves an abstraction of a description (both structural and functional), so the language may support modeling but cannot be just 'for' modeling. As with natural languages, this system language is meant to facilitate communications between people, who, after all, are forming mental models based on a language.

The third element of my efforts was to show how to use such a language to conduct a much more in-depth systems analysis of real systems. The first part of my book describes a more holistic, structured, and formal method of systems analysis that is needed to truly gain understanding of concrete complex, dynamic systems. Systems analysis, as currently practiced in, for example, the development of information systems (so-called software engineering), is extremely ad hoc and not properly oriented toward the whole system of work processes for which the information system is supposed to act as support. The methods employed are based on ideas of best practices rather than principles of systems. The typical approach is to 'ask the users what their requirements are (requirements gathering). All too often users (whatever that means) actually don't really understand their own 'needs' vs. what they believe they want. Today, the number, kinds, and severity of system design failures may be traced back to the lack of adequate analysis of the actual system being serviced by the information subsystem. Moreover, a lack of a truly comprehensive model of management decision making (the basis of the need for an information system in the first place) almost certainly guarantees that designed systems will fail somewhere. In the book I show how a complete analysis based on whole systems principles leads to the successful capture of knowledge needed to produce models and design specifications.

From my interactions with the SRT I began realizing that the concept of a language needed more definition than just a set of lexical elements and a syntax. Subsequently, I have been investigating the development of an ontological approach to substantiating the lexicon as well as how to use that basic ontology as a base language extensible into specific knowledge domains. I want to thank David Rousseau and his colleagues particularly for prompting my thinking in this direction.

The Linz Results from My Perspective

The SRT was able to outline a possible process whereby a product, a portfolio of systems science research conceptual and methodological frameworks, tools, and techniques, etc. could be produced and offered to a range of researchers. These researchers may be working specifically on systems science as the domain of interest or in one of the many physical and social science domains that need systems approaches (e.g. systems biology).

A collateral theme of the Conversation was: How can systems research support the growth of systems literacy in society? Peter Tuddenham has been working on developing a program for the development of systems literacy similar to the one he worked on for Ocean Literacy and he presented his program early in the week so we would keep this theme in mind. He presented our team with some ideas of how we might orient our efforts to support this work. It is clearly a very important part of raising systems thinking throughout society and finding ways to support systems research would seem to be a natural way to do so. My impression, however, is that exactly how this would work is not yet understood (except in general terms). The plan is to continue exploring this connection.

Throughout the week ideas were advanced and discussed. Concepts about what is going to be needed to increase the general awareness of systemness as a way to view the world emerged. A general process model of what would need to be 'done' and how it would be done was suggested by Andreas Hieronymi and developed by the team members. Ray Ison presented ideas for how to conceptualize the product set that would work through this process model, calling it a "portfolio of investments". So the notion of a product and a process for producing and delivering it, along with follow up through feedback from monitoring how the products were effective in their social impact also emerged in my understanding.

By the end of the week we were left with an outline vision of what needed to be done. I characterized what we had accomplished as the product of an early phase of an "agile" analysis method.

We have to admit that Agile Methods have become increasingly popular in several systems engineering domains. However, one characterization of agile methods is that they recognize the futility of trying to define systems up front. In fact the problem lay in the methods of analysis that are generally employed in attempting to get system requirements. They are extraordinarily weak and most of the failures of systems derive from the lack of adequate analysis. This problem still exists within the agile methods but is compensated for by having a user actually participate in an iterative construction through refinement process. A recent survey of software system fails indicates that the rates of failure of projects has not really improved over the old so-called waterfall model.

At this juncture it is incumbent on those interested in continuing and refining this work to analyze exactly what the proposed process would entail. Several important questions need answering. For example: Are the identified component sub-processes sufficient, necessary, or even correctly identified? Another very important question involves the assumptions used to envision this portfolio itself.

As an example, for myself, I focused on the assumption that systems researchers need a much better language of systems for the purposes of doing this exact kind of analysis; a language that covers the 'upper' ontology of general systems and provides a basis for constructing simulation models. Thus, to me, the portfolio should include this language and a set of support tools for conducting systems analysis and modeling. In a paper presented at ISSS-16 I explained how current languages, such as system dynamics, are limited subsets of the full ontology of general systems and are therefore inadequate for tackling the very complex systems that the sciences are now interested in.

Conducting a systems analysis on our presumptive system process would seem to be a natural approach. In doing this we will address the questions above and many more. Moreover, we will be able to share understanding about what is going on and how to proceed. The SA of the LoSK process would naturally lead to the design of the system and provide the basis of a systems engineering approach to constructing an actual process. I presume the IFSR will be able to provide guidance as to how to actually follow through with implementation.

Method

I am proposing to use the language of systems that I presented in July at ISSS Boulder and the methodology of rigorous SA to determine what the currently identified components are supposed to do, and how they relate to one another. This method produces a set of system maps at each level of deconstruction. It also produces a knowledgebase of what each element of the map is and its input/output relations to the other elements.

Systems Analysis Overview

This section will describe the general procedure of systems analysis applied to a to-be-developed process that is supposed to produce a particular product. The very same methods can be applied to existing natural or artificial systems precisely because the principles of systemness apply to all. However, there are particular problems associated with the creative process needed to 'invent' a new process system. In such a case the analysis process actually involves generating imaginative models as part of the deconstruction process.

SA consists of three basic phases. The first phase involves identification of the system of interest (SOI) which includes determining the boundaries of the SOI. This is, in itself, a sometimes arduous task but it is absolutely essential to determine. Part of that activity involves identifying boundary characteristics and the interactions the SOI has with entities in its environment (sources and sinks for flows). The analysis of the SOI's interactions with its environment constitutes determining its behavior under variations in the flows. While the various entities that act as sources and sinks are not analyzed for their internals, the characteristics of the flows, e.g. what substance, how much, modulation characteristics, etc. do need to be analyzed.

corresponds to the 'observational' phase of sciences such as taxonomy, astronomy, and others where tools for exploring internal details are lacking. Input and output flows are traced back to their source/sink entities or external stocks.

The second phase consists of the deconstruction of the SOI into its component subsystems and determining the internal flows of substances between them (figures 2 and 3). In the SRT effort we came to a point of identifying a number of internal components or factors considered important for the production of the portfolio product. We did not, however consider how these might be thought of as subsystems or how substances flowed between them. I will present some ideas on how to proceed below.

This second phase has two stages. The first stage is to identify the subsystems and the second is to identify the internal flows.

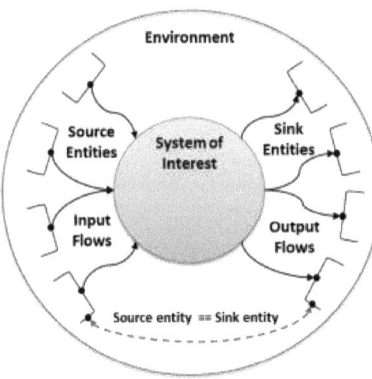

Fig. 1. **Phase 1 of SA.**

Fig 1 shows Phase 1 of SA. This involves identifying the system of interest, its interactions with its direct environment, and its behavior within that environment. Flows (arrows) in this figure are generic. They are normally identified as matter, energy, or messages (which can carry information) with their flow characteristics (volumes, gradients, etc.). By convention sources are put on the left and sinks on the right. If an entity is both (bottom pair) it is represented by two (or more) entities with an indicated linkage. Source and sink entities are represented by open rectangles.

This phase seeks to characterize the behavior of the SOI given the fluctuations in flows into and out of the SOI over time. This

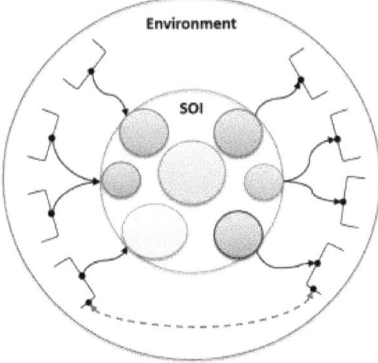

Fig. 2. **The first activity in SOI deconstruction identifies the internal subsystems and free components (atomic subsystems if any). The input flows from the environment are mapped to the receiving/exporting subsystems.**

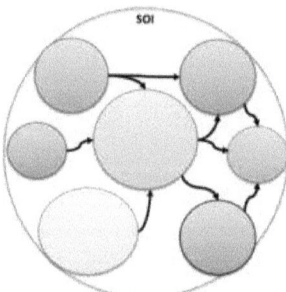

Fig. 3. Flows between subsystems are identified and mapped. Matter and energy conservation laws are observed to account for all flow substances.

The third phase is actually a recursive repetition of the first two phases. In this regard we select one particular subsystem to be a new SOI but at a lower level of organization. We treat this new SOI in the same way we did the original SOI. The other subsystems in the original SOI with which the new SOI interacts now become the source and sink entities in the new one's environment. Thus an analysis of the new SOI's environment is conducted similarly to that of the original whole system. This is followed by the second phase applied to the deconstruction of the new SOI, again in exactly the same way we came up with the subsystems of the original system. An infinite recursion is prevented by finding a level of organization in which the subsystems are 'atomic' processes (simplest possible processes, defined in the procedure).

All of the original subsystems are analyzed in exactly the same way. Throughout the analysis discovered items are coded (example below) in a way that allows reconstruction of maps and organization trees (levels of organization) and the data is collected on the structures and functions internal to the system. The data is entered into a structured database design, a knowledgebase that is derived from the mathematical definition of system. The analysis can use mathematical methods, for example flow network analysis, to check on consistencies and balances (e.g. first and second laws of thermodynamics used to keep track of all energy flows).

It should be noted that the direction of analysis can and often will be reversed to work from the inside back toward the outside; that is into the environment. This can happen when, for example, a flow discovered inside the original SOI cannot be accounted for from the sum of the inflows from entity sources. It is necessary to backtrack to the environment analysis to see what was missed. Or an environmental entity will cease behaving as it had historically leading to inconsistencies in the SOI. It could be necessary to broaden the original boundary of the analysis (not the SOI's boundary) to include a SA performed on that changed entity. In doing so it is possible to recognize a new 'meta-system' to consider as the SOI.

Indeed, the inclusion of environmental entities in an outward analysis can lead to understanding super-systems. For example, the analysis of a single commercial organization could be expanded to analyze the whole industry in which that organization competes by treating all similar organizations as part of the larger system (a new super-SOI) embedded in the yet larger economic environment. Mathematically, this outward analysis is characterized by recognizing the root of a hierarchy tree (the original SOI) as having a parent node, the super-SOI.

Application to the Proposed SRT Proposed Process

Establishing the Context

Systems analysis is typically a top-down process of deconstruction (decomposition) that seeks to preserve functional and structural relations between components discovered. It is therefore necessary to start the analysis by establishing the context in which the system of interest (SOI) operates. In this analysis I will start much further out from the SOI in order to establish the context and motivation for wanting the world to become more systems literate.

This section is extracted from another book project waiting in the wings till the "Understanding" book is completed. That future work is tentatively titled, "The World System." The intent had been to analyze the human social system using systems analysis in order to better understand the human condition and its relations to the rest of the Ecos.

The Big Picture – The Human Social System in the Ecos

What follows is a short sequence of figures meant to situate the effort of the team in a much larger attempt to understand the human social system (HSS) as it is embedded in the Ecos. Figure 9 sets up the basic problem. The Earth is essentially a closed system with respect to material flows but open to energy. The flow of energy through the Ecos drives the work processes that create the living environment and provide the motive forces for auto-organization, emergence, and evolution of higher orders of organization.

The human social system (HSS, in figure 4), the most complex subsystem within the Ecos, is a wholly owned subsidiary of the Ecos and not the other way around – in my value system. Based on the evidence to date this may be true in an objective sense as well.

It has been estimated that the HSS now accounts for more than 40% of primary productivity on the planet and is consuming fossil sun light at unsustainable rates. Clearly the HSS is "out of control" with respect to its confiscation of the Ecos' natural resources. This cannot go on indefinitely. One of the major contributions to the HSS and the Ecos of systems science is to provide the scientific platform for understanding how all of this works and exploring the application of governance to keep the HSS in some dynamic balance with the rest of the Ecos.

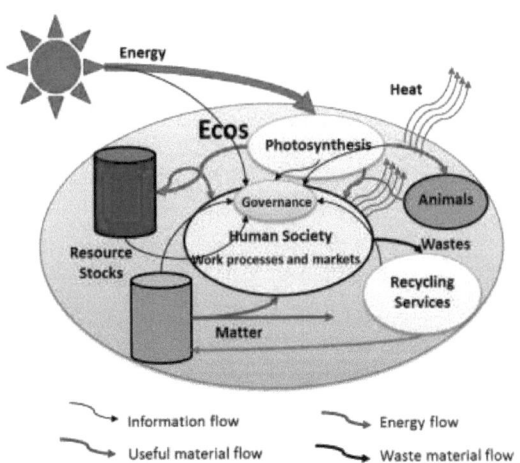

Fig. 4. **The HSS is a subsystem of the whole Earth ecological supra-system, the Ecos.**

The HSS is a messy affair when observed casually (figure 5). A lot of the messiness derives from the fact that humans participate in multiple different activities at different times in the diurnal cycle (temporal multiplexing) as well as over their lives. Those activities, however, are within larger subsystems that work to provide humanity with its means of living on the planet. This figure examines the modern situation that has evolved over the last 10,000 years or so. In my book, "Understanding the Human Social System," (in progress) I provide an evolutionary model of the development of the HSS to its modern form. Here I just introduce it in preparation for parsing the bit which is of interest to our current project, "Science and Engineering." The Venn diagram suggests that the HSS is composed of a number of fuzzy bounded subsystems all of which include human participation. In fact, the way systems are defined, these subsystems are technically fuzzy sets using a membership function that includes a temporal function.

The Human Social System Delineated

Figure 5 does not attempt to capture all relevant subsystems in the HSS, though I would argue it captures some of the most significant. The overlap between subsystems represents the fact that many of them strongly interact with one another (strongly coupled) and share component sub-subsystems, principally human beings as they participate in different roles. Human biology/psychology is at the core and overlaps with everything (circle in the center labeled 'Humans'). The other subsystems exist to support human life in some state of affluence (at least ideally). Humans move in and out of functions within each subsystem. For example, humans may enter the Healthcare system as patients or as healthcare providers at different times.

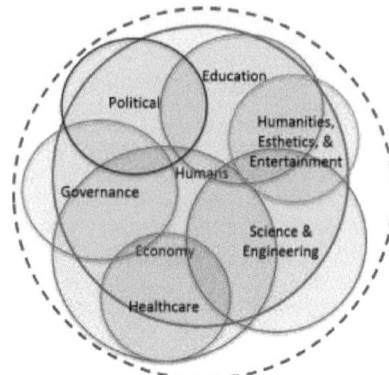

Fig. 5. The HSS is a 'messy' set of subsystems organized around the core human biology/psychology.

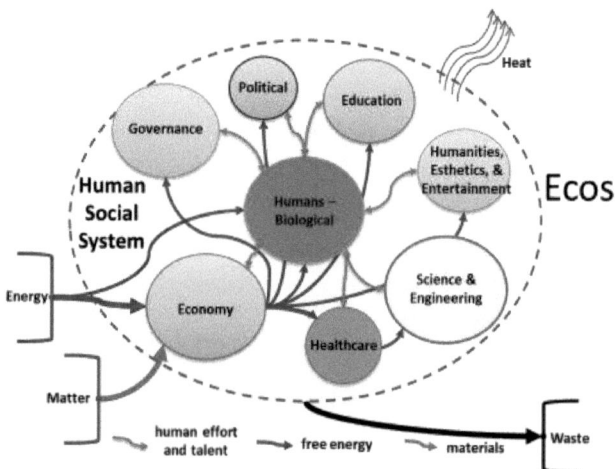

Fig. 6. Defuzzification of the map in figure 5 is accomplished by delineating the flow paths and relations between the subsystems. This map shows internal flows, for example, of energy obtained through economic activity and provided to other subsystem.

Figure 6 looks at the subsystems after a defuzzification operation that includes taking time into account. Humans are shown as flowing out of the merely biological sphere into and out of the other processes and back to the biological reality of existence (two headed orange arrows).

The Science & Technology process is not colored since this is the process I wish to deconstruct shortly. The heat radiation symbol at the top shows the concern for natural laws such as the second law of thermodynamics in this kind of analysis. Not shown is another concern for the conservation of matter, which would be realized in recycling operations within the HSS. The objective of such a subsystem would be to minimize the waste material exported to the environment.

The Science & Engineering Subsystem Delineated

Figure 7 shows a simplified system map of the S&E subsystem. This figure abstracts considerably, for example all of the other HSS components besides Education and Humans have been collapsed into a single representation in order to simplify the diagram.

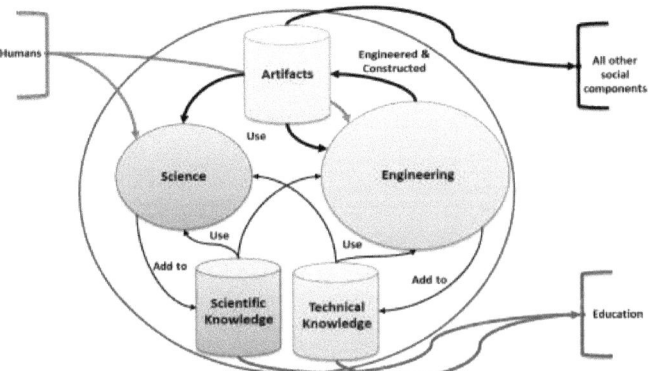

Fig. 7. This diagram shows a very simplified representation of the S&E subsystem of the HSS.

Science and Engineering represent a strongly coupled set of component sub-processes. Even though strongly coupled, each has its own focal function that produces several critical output products for society. Two of the most important products are shown here, artifacts (e.g. technology), and accessible knowledge (information shown flowing out to the Education subsystem as well as feeding back to the two internal sub-processes).

The inputs shown here are people, scientists and engineers who have already been affected by the Education subsystem and are the 'laborers' participating in the S&E system. This figure is just to further establish the context of the LoSK process which, through its portfolio product, will begin to modify the inputs to this system.

This is the context for doing the SA of the LoSK process. I now situate the Science subsystem as the SOI and show a presumptive influence of the LoSK product, the portfolio, on the "normal" science process.

The Normal Science Process

Normal, here, means the way in which science is working today, taking into account its evolutionary history over the last 500+ years. I won't be going into all of the aspects of the science process. Figure 8 is another cartoon representation of this subsystem meant to refine the context of the LoSK process. Here I represent science as practiced in modern disciplinary silos, where the typical pattern of behavior is what we have often called reductionist science. The scientist is drilling down to explain a phenomenon as if it is all that mattered.

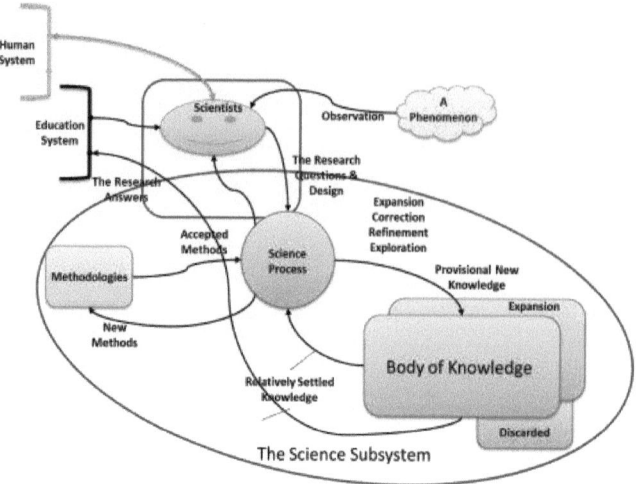

Fig. 8. The "normal" science process involves trained scientists acting in the interface, observing a phenomenon of interest and then working through established methodologies (or sometimes exploring new methodologies) to increase our knowledge of the world and how the phenomenon of interest fits into that world.

Presumed Effect of Systems Science Influence on Normal Science

Having seen the impacts of systems thinking applied to many disciplines over the last several decades, it is presumed that a more rigorous application of systems science would strongly influence the effectiveness of multi-disciplinary science work. One such effect might be to enable disciplinary scientists to become more holistic in their thinking about how their phenomenon of interests interrelates to other phenomena in the world. The system map in figure 9 attempts to demonstrate what the impact of a rigorous systems science process would be and how that process could interact with the normal science process to affect the thinking.

Other influences on normal science would include the use of specific tools and techniques which are designed to provide rigorous systems analysis and design of experiments as well as general understanding of how phenomena studied fit into the larger body of knowledge for the field as well as the integrated body of knowledge for all fields.

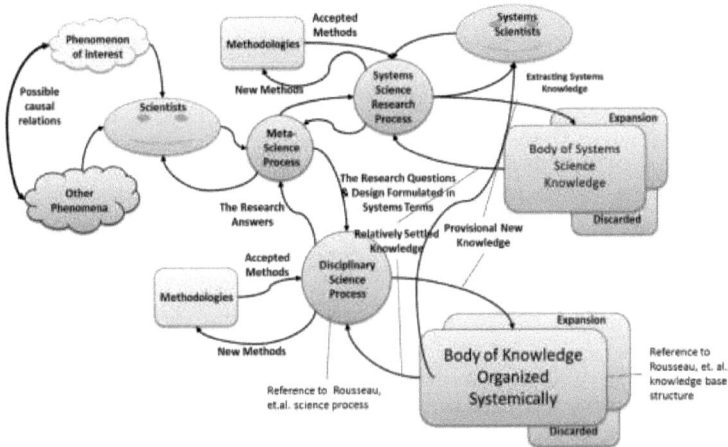

Fig. 9. Through the construction of a formal systems science research process and interfacing it with the disciplinary science process through a "meta-science" process, disciplinary scientists will have the wherewithal to think more holistically and, presumably, communicate better with scientists from other disciplines in multi-disciplinary projects.

Integrating the Model with the SRT Flow of Influence Model

Figure 10 attempts to integrate the model of flow of influence presented by Andreas with the model above. The top part shows the basic "Toward Systems Literacy" model (see Final Report (10 page), figure 2). The bottom part shows a simplified process model that would result from the efforts to generate the portfolio output (leftmost blue arrow in the upper part). The oval labeled "Systems Science Process" corresponds with the "Systems Science Research Process" oval in figure 9 above.

Thus we can begin to focus in on the real system of interest in this effort, the Landscape of Systems Knowing process.

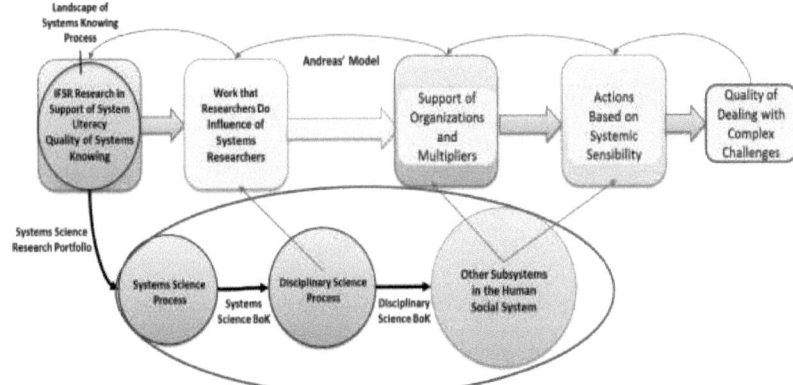

Fig. 10 LoSK-process

Fig. 10. Shows how the LoSK process (deep blue box/oval at left) creates the flow of influence in the model. The lower oval represents the entire process whereby the influences of systems literacy (the systems body of knowledge) begins to impact the practice of science and engineering in society and thus the overall quality of transdisciplinary research.

Analysis of the LoSK Process
Structural and Functional Deconstruction

Starting from the mind map created in Linz model (see Final Report (10 page), table 1 and figure 3), I have constructed a first level deconstruction map of the process. In figure 11 I show the first stage in the second phase of SA, the components designated as critical factors in the SRT report. I have added one additional "critical factor" or subsystem, the "Production Export" function that is the subsystem that will assemble the portfolio and publish it.

In the figure are also shown a few sources and sinks with flows demonstrating how to work with this map in analysis. The objective will be to complete the analysis of the environment (phase 1) and components (as described previously) to verify their inclusion (also to see if there are components needed but not yet identified). The next step would be to identify and map the necessary inputs to each component in terms of inputs from the external environment (external sources) as well as inputs from the other components. Likewise, we need to identify the outputs and their flows to other components or to external sinks. This analysis is an iterative process in which each "champion" of a component will treat theirs as a system of interest focusing strictly on the inputs and outputs needed (to the best of their knowledge) for that component to process its product(s). We then go through a process of integration that will result in a top level map of the LoSK process.

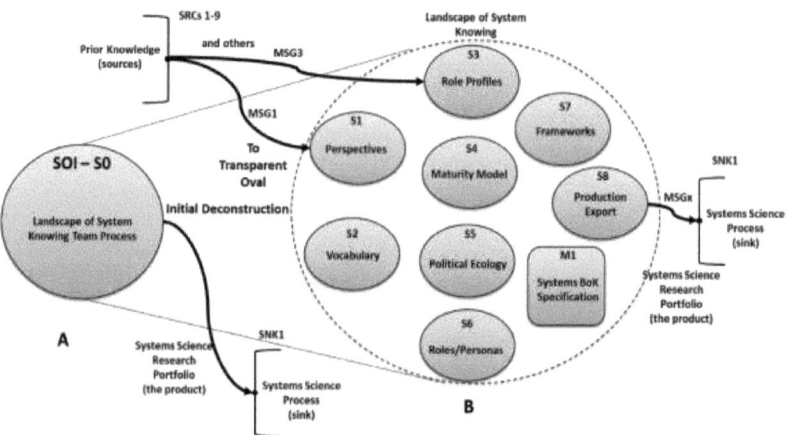

Fig. 11. The first steps in deconstructing the structures and functions of the LoSK process involves mapping the inputs and outputs. A) Looking at the LoSK process at the top level, coded 'S0'. B) Identifying a few inputs, the internal subsystems, and the same output as shown in A.

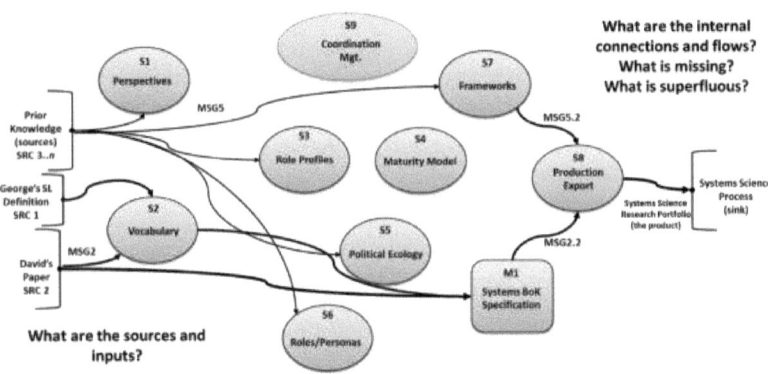

Fig. 12. The next step in deconstruction is to open up the LoSK system and ask some crucial questions.

Table 1 lists the components thus far identified. The columns Champion Name and Description are left open (except where I have volunteered) awaiting others in the SRT who are proponents of specific components to take charge of developing that component. I have put my name in the "Vocabulary" row as a starter. Below I will show some examples of next steps in developing this model further.

Table 1. Assignment of Champions and descriptions of these components.

Component ID	Name	Champion Name	Description
S1	Perspectives		
S2	Vocabulary [Ontology/Language]	George Mobus	Defining a systems language (ontology) for purposes of supporting systems analysis and design. See Mobus, 2016.
S3	Role Profiles		
S4	Maturity Model		
S5	Political Ecology		
S6	Roles/Personas		
S7	Frameworks		
S8	Production/Export		
S9	Coordination Management		
M1	Systems BoK Specification		

An Example Deconstruction of one Subsystem

In this example I am assuming the role of champion (principal stakeholder) for what we have named the "Vocabulary" component. As I indicated in Linz, I have already been at work on developing an ontology and language of systems that I think will work to support numerous systems-oriented research. I will present a paper in Boulder that will introduce the language and its basis in a formal definition of system. SRC 1, in figure 13, below, is proposed to be the definition of this language in which the lexicon and syntax constitute at least a set of vocabulary primitives. These primitives ground the specific terminology of a discipline through a developed typology (ontology). For example, the language provides a basis for defining a boundary for the SOI whether it is conceptual or real. The boundary can be called a 'cell membrane' or a 'membership function' (for fuzzy systems) depending on the investigator's POV and research question(s).

Process S2 should identify the useful elements of a language of systems to be used by researchers doing systems analysis and design. The language should provide a universal systems ontology, terms, syntax, and semantics that can be applied to all systems and thus be a common language that can be spoken by researchers from every discipline. The product would come in the form of a language specification (upper ontology for systems science) and a user's manual that guides researchers (both systems and disciplinary) and engineers in using the language to perform systems analysis and design.

Below is a rough, preliminary example of a use of the language to analyze and construct a model of the process that is supposed to produce this product. The other seven critical elements would be produced by similar processes. What I am proposing to do is to follow this formal procedure to identify the internals of all of those processes (and their products) so that other members of the team can become familiar with this procedure (in the absence of an existing ontology specification and language user's manual!)

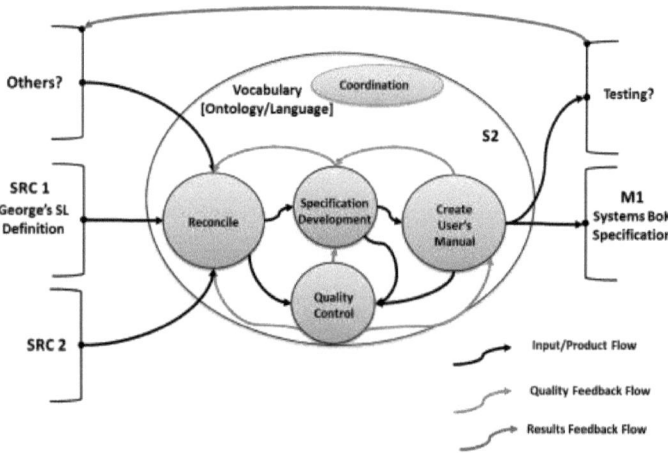

Fig. 13. A quick-and-dirty pass at deconstruction of the Vocabulary (definition) subsystem. Pathways for inputs and outputs are shown. As with all such development projects the product at each stage of production is reviewed for quality (TBD) and feedback is used to assure the products meet standards. The process is monitored and coordinated explicitly (message flows not shown). The coordinator also communicates with external entities.

Source Inputs
- **SRC 1: SL Definition**
  - Definition of system
  - Ontology of Systemness
  - Lexicon, Syntax, Semantics
- **SRC 2: Rousseau, et al, Paper**
  - In Search of General Systems Theory
- **Others?**
  - Any other possible stakeholder inputs
  - Any other sources of knowledge inputs needed
  - Evaluator of testing (TBD)

Sink Outputs
- **M1: Systems BoK Language Specification**
  - Final language specification sent to the repository BoK to become part of the portfolio.
- **Testing**
  - Language specification in its test format sent for external review/testing, essentially a user acceptance.
  - Feedback from the testing sink provide input as needed.

Subsystems
- **Reconcile**
  - Takes in the three inputs (above) and works to reconcile and integrate perspectives. Will also get feedback from testing to guide corrections or additions/deletions of language issues.
  - Acts to identify and specify 'user' needs.
- **Specification Development**
  - Works to structure the ontology, etc. into a standard language explication (e.g. like a programming language description document.
  - Produces the language, etc. specification.
- **Create User's Manual**
  - Works to produce a manual explaining to users how they will use the language for the purposes of analysis and modeling.
- **Quality Control**
  - Internal 'unit' testing and editing to assure the quality of the systems language specification.
  - Identifies issues and sends discrepancies back to appropriate stage for correcting.
- **Coordination**
  - The 'systems engineering process that monitors progress, provides internal coordination between above processes.
  - Communicates with external entities and determines other sources as needed.

This process is essentially a systems development process that takes as its input the existing ontology along with any other likely ontology candidates (not thought of) and produces the provisional language specification and user's manual (how to use the language). The process may be implemented by a team with one member designated as a coordinator. The final product will be tested by user stakeholders in order to assure usefulness. Once approved it can be transferred to the BoK process for incorporation into the portfolio.

Background on Deriving Systemese

The method by which Kalton and I developed our systems ontology, lexical elements, and syntax for systemese is diagrammed in figure 14.

This process was used over several decades in an informal manner. Mobus and Kalton were involved in surveys of real systems analyzing the similarities of attributes and features. Recently I have attempted to make it more formal (as per the figure) so that more people might get involved in deriving ontological terms, etc.

This cursory review of the SA process applied to one of the components of the SRT LoSK process, the 'vocabulary' development process, I hope, will show essentially how SA can be applied to the other components and the whole process. Doing this kind of analysis should help define more rigorously the whole system shown in figure 10 above.

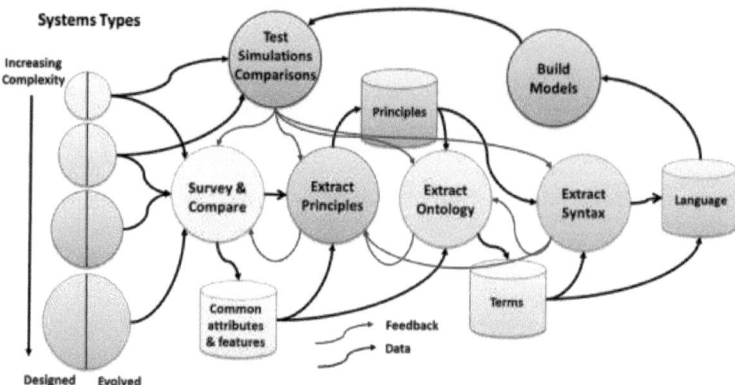

Fig. 14. The process for developing a system language involves extracting system models from a survey of real world (System Types) at various levels of complexity, both designed systems and natural (evolved) ones. The 'Principles' named in Mobus & Kalton (2015) were found to apply across the survey of systems. I began work on an ontology, set of terms naming things and relations in systems, and a syntax for forming valid statements about systems. These efforts are being used to define a language of system.

Next Steps

Subsequent to the Linz Conversation and a follow up meeting at the ISSS-Boulder conference it appears that there is momentum toward producing the process for producing the portfolio product. My proposal had been to conduct a systems analysis of this process in the manner shown in the prior section. Others have been working on additional definitions/descriptions of some of the other eight components identified in Linz so a basis for further analysis is starting to take shape.

Several questions need to be resolved. For one, what do we imagine the embodiment of this process would be? There is a strong sense in which this process constitutes an integrated whole system; all of the parts may need to be developed in a coordinated way in order to achieve the goals. This implies a unified organization with clear communications between all of the components. Will the IFSR set up an "office" staffed with people to run the process of producing portfolio items? Will this be designed as a virtual organization to be handed off to some other organization for realization? Could it be handled as an open source process with the IFSR providing the platform? Who would the people be doing the work when it is realized?

These kinds of question raise additional questions regarding financing of the construction and operations of this organization. A physical space in which people are doing the work, the "office", would require both capital and operations financing. I am not sure the production of the elements of the portfolio will generate significant income so the operations budgets will need to be financed by grants. If this is set up as an open source process far less financing would be needed however there is still a significant cost of managing the process. Would this be supplied by volunteer work as happens in the Linux open source operating system projects?

These are the kinds of questions that would be addressed as part of the systems analysis process I am proposing. They are the kinds of questions you find answered in, for example, a pro forma plan. Perhaps the members of the SRT who are involved in commercial types of systems work could provide this component.

If we can identify the individuals who will take on the responsibilities (i.e. fill in names in Table 1) I can take responsibility for working with them on doing further environment and deconstruction analysis to flesh out the workings of this LoSK portfolio production system. Could someone from the world of commercial systems step up to work on answering some of these "business" pro forma questions?

Addendum

After writing this report there has developed a proposal for many of the principals in the SRT and in the Systems Literacy groups along with members of the INCOSE SSWG to meet within the INCOSE Workshop in January, 2017. There are a number of people across the several organizations who have a similar interest in producing what amounts to a SS BoK that would find use not only in systems science research but in systems engineering. It would be nice if some of these ideas can be further discussed and we come away from that meeting with firmer plans for next steps.

Acknowledgements

My sincerest thanks to the members of the Systems Research Team who have helped me think more clearly about the nature of the problem to be solved and provided a number of approaches to its solution. The ideas presented below are, I believe, greatly strengthened by the week in Linz. Any defects I will take credit for.

What are IFSR Conversations?

Conversations were introduced by Bela H. Banathy around 1980 as an alternative to the classical conferences which usually consist only of presentation of streamlined papers and short question slots. In a Conversation a small group of scientists meets for several days to discuss in a self-guided way a topic of scientific and social importance. A Conversation is preceded by an intensive preparation phase and followed by a post-conversation consolidation period. No papers are presented during the conversation; the participants discuss face-to-face their topic, often modifying it in the course of the conversation.

Bela Banathy always considered conversation as a "future creating disciplined inquiry" (Banathy, 1996, p. 45) when engaged with in the spirit of social systems design (SSD).

The first conversation took place at the Fuschl Lake in Austria in April 1982. A group of systems scholars met in a small hotel at the Fuschl Lake, near Salzburg. Participants came from three continents, representing ten cultures.

From 1981 onwards the IFSR together with the ISI has organized one IFSR Conversation every other year, originally in a hotel in Fuschl, near Salzburg (hence they were known as "Fuschl Conversations). When Bela Banathy stopped attending the Fuschl Conversations the ISI gradually ceased to operate as the primary organizer of the Conversation Events, and the IFSR with Gerhard Chroust as Secretary General took over all aspects of the sponsorship and running of the Fuschl meetings. This was a natural transition since the IFSR had been providing sponsorship of these events since early on.

In order to improve the meeting facilities the Conversations moved to Pernegg, a small village nearer to Vienna in 2010. In From 2012 onward we chose a seminar hotel in the outskirts of Linz, Austria, resulting in an even better environment for the conversation.

In parallel additional Conversations were organized by IFSR's member organizations in many locations around the world. The various conversations that followed the first Fuschl event, have been organized and coordinated by the International Systems Institute, in cooperation with International Federation of Systems Research, and with several member organizations of the Federation. By now we [the ISI] have held thirty conversations; ten Conversations in Fuschl, Austria; eight regional conversations: two in Crete; one each in England, Finland, Greece, Hungary; and three in Spain. Since 1989, we have held twelve international Conversations at the Asilomar Conference Center in California and established the Asilomar Conversation Community (ACC) as a conversation community of the International Systems Institute. Conversations of the ISI continue to be held in other Conversaciones del Extremo Sur which began in 2012 in the southern most city of the world, Ushuaia, Argentina,

In their book on Dialogue as a Collective Means of Design Conversation (2008), editors Patrick Jenlink and Bela Banathy provide a brief history of the Conversation Movement.

The proceedings from these Conversation, starting with 1996, can be found on the IFSR homepage (http://www.ifsr.org/index.php/category/archives/proceedings-of-ifsr-conversations).

References:
Banathy, Bela H., 1996 Designing Social Systems in a Changing World. Plenum, 1996.
Gordon Dyer : Guidebook for Designing and Sustaining Effective Conversation, version 8, December 2016
 [http://www.ifsr.org/wp-content/uploads/2016/02/guide-effective-conversation_V8_DEC16.pdf]

Gordon Dyer : Guidebook for Designing and Sustaining Effective Conversation - ADDENDUM for Team Leaders, , version 6, December 2016 [http://www.ifsr.org/wp-content/uploads/2016/02/guide-effective-conversation-TEAMLEADERS_V6_DEC16.pdf]

IFSR (ed.)(1996 Fuschl Conversation 1998: IFSR Newsletter, October 1996 vol. 15, no. 3 (No. 42), pp, 1-2

IFSR (ed.) (2010) Why Conversation and what form do they take? IFSR Newsletter, vol. 27 (2010), no. 1, p. 6
IFSR - International Federation for Systems Research, Linz, and http://www.ifsr.org/index.php/ifsr-newsletter-2010-vol27-no1-june/

ISI (ed.) The International Systems Institute http://www.systemsinstitute.com/about-2/the-isi-story

Jenlink, Patrick and Banathy, Bela H. Dialogue as a Collective Means of Design Conversation (volume 2). Springer, 2008.

Laszlo A. 2012 And A Brief Background on the Fuschl Conversations , IFSR Newsletter, Volume 30, no. 1 (December 2013) pp. 5 – 7,

Laszlo, Alexander and Krippner, Stanley. Systems Theories: Their origins, foundations, and development. In Jordan, J.S. (ed.) Systems Theories and A Priori Aspects of Perception. Elsevier, 1996.

Laszlo, Alexander and Laszlo, Kathia Castro. The making of a new culture: Learning conversations and design conversations in social evolution. In P.M. Jenlink & B.H. Banathy (Eds.), Dialogue as a Collective Means of Design Conversation. Springer, 2008.

Laszlo, Alexander and Laszlo, Kathia Castro. The evolution of evolutionary systems design. World Futures, 2002, Vol. 58, No. 6-7.

Laszlo, Kathia Castro and Laszlo, Alexander. The conditions for thriving conversations. In B.H. Banathy & P.M. Jenlink (Eds.), Dialogue as a Means for Collective Communication. Kluwer, 2001

Hotel Seewinkel, the original location of the Fuschl/IFSR Conversations (1998)

What is the IFSR?

THE INTERNATIONAL FEDERATION FOR SYSTEMS RESEARCH (IFSR), founded 1981, is a non-profit, scientific and educational organization comprising 45 member organizations (status December 2016) from all continents. The overall purpose of the Federation is to advance cybernetic and systems research and systems applications in order to serve the international systems community (see also its constitution).

The IFSR has shown a healthy growth with respect to the number of members. Currently it has 45 member societies, representing scientists from 25 countries on most continents. For the most recent list see: http://www.ifsr.org/index.php/member-societies/

The Federation is guided by a Board of Directors, composed of two individuals from each member organization. The Board elects a President, one to three Vice Presidents, and the Secretary General. These officers form the Executive Committee (EC). The EC acts for the Board pursuant to the authorization of the Board. The Board meets bi-annually in even years, the EC annually.

The Executive Board of the IFSR
(2016-2018)

President	Vice President	Vice President	Vice President	Secretary General
Dr. Mary C. Edson	Dr. Gary S. Metcalf	Dr. Jennifer Wilby	Prof. Ray Ison	Prof. Gerhard Chroust
USA	USA	UK	UK	AT

Past officers of the IFSR

Year	President	Vice-President(s)	Secretary/Treasurer
1980	George J. Klir	Robert Trappl	Gerard de Zeeuw
1984	Robert Trappl	Bela H. Banathy	Gerard de Zeeuw
1988	Gerrit Broekstra	Franz Pichler	Bela Banathy
1992	Gerard de Zeeuw	J.D.R. De Raadt	Gerhard Chroust
1994	Bela Banathy	Michael C. Jackson	Gerhard Chroust
1998	Michael C. Jackson	Yong Pil Rhee	Gerhard Chroust
2000	Yong Pil Rhee	Michael C. Jackson	Gerhard Chroust
2002	Jifa Gu	Matjaz Mulej, Gary S. Metcalf	Gerhard Chroust
2006	Matjaz Mulej	Jifa Gu, Gary S. Metcalf	Gerhard Chroust
2008	Matjaz Mulej	Yoshiteru Nakamori, Gary S. Metcalf	Gerhard Chroust
2010	Gary S. Metcalf	Kyoichi Jim Kijima, Amanda Gregory, Leonie Solomons	Gerhard Chroust
2012	Gary S. Metcalf	Yoshihide Horiuchi, Stefan Blachfellner	Gerhard Chroust
2014	Gary S. Metcalf	Stefan Blachfellner, Mary C. Edson, Nam Nguyen	Gerhard Chroust
2016	Mary C. Edson	Gary S. Metcalf, Jennifer Wilby, Ray Ison	Gerhard Chroust

Janie Chroust: Seminar hotel St. Magdalena, garden